Sandy Laurie

D0717328

The Methodist Service Book

The Methodist

Service Book

METHODIST
PUBLISHING HOUSE
1975

Words in **bold** type are said by all,
except for words required by law on
pages E5 and E9 of the Marriage
Service.

Printed in Great Britain by
The Garden City Press Limited
Letchworth, Hertfordshire SG6 1JS

7162 0255 7

Contents

Acknowledgements

The texts of the Gloria, the Nicene Creed, the Sanctus, the Benedictus, the Agnus Dei, and the alternative versions of the Apostles' Creed are reproduced by permission of the International Consultation on English Texts.

Biblical passages are from the *Revised Standard Version*, © 1946 and 1952, Division of Christian Education of the National Council of the Churches of Christ in the United States of America.

The Confession of Sin, the wording of the petitions in Intercession A, the Easter Preface in Thanksgiving B, in the Sunday Service, are from the Order for Holy Communion Series 3 by permission of the Registrars of the Provinces of Canterbury and York.

Intercessions B and C and Thanksgivings B and D in the Sunday Service are adapted by permission from Prayer Book Studies 21: The Holy Eucharist, © Charles Mortimer Guilbert, 1970, as custodian of the Standard Book of Common Prayer, Church Hymnal Corporation, 800 Second Avenue, New York.

Intercession D in the Sunday Service is adapted by permission of the Provincial Secretary of the Church of the Province of New Zealand. Thanksgiving C is adapted from Stephen F. Winward, *Responsive Service Book* (Hodder and Stoughton) © 1965.

The prayer 'Almighty God, our refuge and strength' on p.F5 is from *A Book of Public Worship* by permission of Oxford University Press (altered by permission).

The prayers 'Father of mercies . . .' and 'Almighty God, always ready to forgive . . .' on pp.F17, F18 are from the *Book of Common Order of the Church of Scotland* by permission of the Committee on Public Worship and Aids to Devotion of the Church of Scotland (amended).

The prayer 'Merciful God, our heavenly Father' on p.F16 is reproduced, with slight revisions, from *Alternative Services, Second Series* by permission of the Registrars of the Provinces of Canterbury and York.

The prayer 'May God in his infinite love and mercy . . .' on p.F18 is from *Prayer and the Departed* by permission of the Registrars of the Provinces of Canterbury and York.

The prayer 'Holy Father, grant us, in all our duties . . .' on p.F17 is from *Parish Prayers* by Frank Colquhoun (Hodder and Stoughton).

Preface

In 1784 John Wesley published *The Sunday Service of the Methodists in North America, with other occasional Services*. Its Preface began with this sentence: 'I believe there is no Liturgy in the world, either in ancient or in modern language, which breathes more of a solid, scriptural rational piety than the Common Prayer of the Church of England.' He goes on to say that little alteration is made in the following edition of it, except in certain instances, which he specifies. Further editions followed, some of them for the Methodists of Great Britain, who after his death continued to commend the use of 'our venerable father's Abridgement'. The books which have since been produced by the branches of Methodism in Great Britain and throughout the world are all indebted to it. After the union of British Methodism in 1932, the Conference authorized *The Book of Offices* of 1936. Its preface contains the sentence: 'It must not be thought that there is here any attempt to disparage the practice of free prayer, which has always been one of the glories of Methodism', and goes on to say, 'There is no real conflict between free prayer and liturgical prayer, for the most fervent and the most helpful prayers that ever came from the inspiration of the moment will be found to owe much in their expression to the remembrance of the language of the great liturgies, and of the hymns of Methodism.'

Now after nearly forty years another Service Book is presented to the Methodist people. These forms are not intended, any more than those in earlier books, to curb creative freedom, but rather to provide norms for its guidance. The ecumenical movement has brought Methodists into close contact with the worship of other communions; and though this book resembles the Book of Common Prayer less than any of its predecessors, it will serve as a link not only with the Church of England but with other communions also, for the investigations of liturgical scholars into the origins and basic structures of liturgical rites have caused a marked convergence in the forms of worship used in various churches. The services retain, however, a distinctively Methodist flavour, and constitute part of our contribution to the life of the universal Church.

In recent years the style and vocabulary of worship have changed considerably. The rich images of the Bible must be retained; but like the Reformers who wrote the Book of Common Prayer, those who lead worship must try to use language which can be understood by the people. Yet where people are attached to the older forms, they should not be deprived of them. For that reason the first service of the Lord's Supper or Holy Communion from *The Book of Offices* of 1936, which is basically that of the Book of Common Prayer, 1662, and in which God is addressed as 'thou', has been retained along with the new form of this service.

The title 'The Sunday Service', which John Wesley used in a somewhat different sense, has been given to two forms of service, one for use when the Lord's Supper is observed, and one for use without the Lord's Supper. The forms are closely related, and much of the material in the appendices, as also the collects, lessons and psalms elsewhere in the book, can be used with either.

This book resembles in its scope the *Shorter Book of Offices* rather than the full book. The custom of producing a shorter book goes back indeed to 1839. It omits, among other things, the Order of Morning Prayer (which was printed with, but was not strictly part of, *The Book of Offices*), the Ordination of Deaconesses and other services of Recognition and Dedication. The Conference will be asked in due course to authorize revised versions of these services also, and they will carry the same authority as if they were bound within the same covers, as indeed some day they may be. It is simply for practical convenience that the Service Book is published in this short form. The book contains no forms for daily devotions, whether for family or for individual use. *The Daily Office*, published by the Joint Liturgical Group, and the various schemes of Bible readings supply this need so well that it has not been thought necessary to provide other forms.

The book, moreover, contains the traditional as well as the modern forms of the Apostles' Creed, the Nicene Creed, the hymns 'Glory be to God on high' and 'Holy, holy, holy, Lord God of hosts', and the traditional forms may be substituted for the modern ones in any of the services. Congregations need not hesitate to use the traditional forms, just as it is to be hoped that they will long continue to use Charles Wesley's hymns. The words of the Lord's Prayer are not printed in the text of the services, but elsewhere in the book a version of the traditional form and a modern form have been printed, with a note as to their use.

In the preparation of this book other Methodist Conferences and the churches of other communions have been extensively consulted, and the experimental versions of these services have been widely used throughout British Methodism for several years. May the fruit of all this endeavour be to the glory of God and the building up of his people in love.

Entry into the Church

Baptism

General Directions

1 The Font should, when possible, stand prominently in a space apart.

2 The church stewards shall see that all necessary arrangements are made for the administration of the Sacrament of Baptism, after due notice has been given to the Minister, in the case of children by the parents or guardians, in other cases by the candidate for Baptism.

3 Before or during the service water shall be poured into the Font.

4 The Minister shall enquire beforehand whether each candidate has already been baptized.

5 No one shall be baptized who is known to have been baptized already.

6 If it is uncertain whether a candidate has already been baptized, the following form of words is to be used at the Baptism:
> *N.*, if you are not already baptized, I baptize you in the Name of the Father, and of the Son, and of the Holy Spirit. **Amen.**

7 It is fitting that water should be poured or sprinkled upon the candidate three times or that he should be dipped in the water three times, once at the mention of each Person of the Trinity, but it is sufficient that it be done once.

8   The officiating Minister shall see that Baptisms, whether public or private, are entered in the Register of Baptisms.

The Baptism of Infants

General Directions*

9   A solemn obligation rests upon parents to present their children to Christ in Baptism, which claims for them the benefits of his redeeming work, and signifies their admission into the visible community of his Church. Parents thereby dedicate them to God, and are pledged to bring them up in the nurture and admonition of the Lord; and the Sacrament of Baptism is administered on their promise so to do.

10 Before every administration of Baptism at least seven days' notice (save in exceptional circumstances) should be required of the parents or guardians to the Minister, in order to permit of interview and preparation.

11 As soon as possible after notice has been given, full enquiry should be made and all necessary instruction and exposition of the service given by the Minister, a Deaconess, or some other competent and instructed Leader. For this purpose the parents or guardians may be visited in their home, or they should be asked to attend at the church at a convenient hour. Instruction

*Cf. *Statement on Holy Baptism* of Conference 1952

should be regarded as particularly necessary in the case of a first child, or of the first Baptism from the home according to the Methodist rite. If the parents or guardians cannot pledge themselves to give the promises contained in the Service of Baptism, the Minister may defer the Baptism of the child.

12 Normally the Sacrament of Baptism should be administered in the church by an ordained Minister, at a service of public worship. Where administration by an ordained Minister is impracticable, the Sacrament may be administered, after consultation with the Superintendent or one of his colleagues, by a Probationary Minister in pastoral charge, by an ordained Deaconess, by a Probationary Deaconess in pastoral charge, or by a fully accredited Local Preacher.

13 This procedure shall be varied only where strong pastoral considerations require that a child presented without proper notice or preparation should not be refused Baptism.

14 Only in cases of prolonged or serious illness should Baptism take place at home or in hospital. On such occasions the Minister, or in emergency any person present, should name the child and pour or sprinkle water upon *him* or dip *him* in water, saying:

> *N.*, I baptize you in the Name of the Father, and of the Son, and of the Holy Spirit. **Amen.**

This is sufficient for Baptism, but it is fitting that all who are present should then say the Lord's Prayer, and that other prayers should be offered as opportunity allows.

15 If the Baptism is administered by any person other than the Minister, notice shall be given at once to the Minister, who shall make the entry in the Register of Baptisms.

16   If the child recovers *he* should be brought to the church in order that the congregation may publicly welcome *him*, preferably at the time when other children are to be baptized. The parents may make the usual answers, except the request for *his* Baptism. The Baptism shall be omitted, and the Minister shall explain to the people that the child has already been received into the congregation of Christ's flock by Baptism. The blessing and the final prayer may be used.

17   The Baptism of infants is normally administered at a main service of public worship. This may well have its own lessons, especially on the principal festivals of the Church, and especially in churches where baptisms are frequent. But otherwise public worship may on some occasions when it includes a baptism have lessons related to Baptism, such as: Genesis 17:1, 7-8; Exodus 19:3-8a; Psalm 42:1-2; Jeremiah 31:31-34; Ezekiel 36:24-28; Acts 2:38-42; Romans 6:3-11; and the Gospel passages in the order of service, viz. Mark 1:9-11; 10:13-16; Matthew 28:18-20. If one of these Gospel passages is read among the lessons, the others are read at the place where they are printed in the service. When baptism for good reason is administered at a service other than the main service of public worship, the lessons and the sermon may be omitted, but the Gospel passages are read.

18   Regular pastoral care shall be given by the local church and its Minister to all who have been baptized, and regular prayer shall be offered for them. A Baptismal Roll shall be kept of all baptized children associated with the church. The officiating Minister shall see that the parents receive a Certificate of Baptism and that particulars of the Baptism are given to the Baptismal Roll Secretary. The Church Family Committee is responsible for the maintenance and periodical review of the Baptismal Roll. It shall satisfy itself that all possible oversight

of baptized children is maintained and suitable instruction given, as they are able to receive it, to prepare them for Christian discipleship.

19   Children who are not yet old enough to answer for themselves may be baptized with the same form of service as is used for infants.

20   Two sponsors may be appointed to assist the parents in carrying out their promises: one chosen by the parents, and the other, who shall normally be a member of the church in which the Baptism takes place, by the Minister.

21   It is the privilege and responsibility of the sponsors to support the parents in the Christian upbringing of the children; to help them to carry out the promises and so to act as a link between the family and the larger family of the church; and regularly to pray for the children.

The Service

The Preparation

1 The Lord's Prayer, if it is not to be said later

2 Any part of the Preparation of the Sunday Service

3 The Collect of the Day, or some other prayer, or this Collect:

> Heavenly Father, we thank you that in every generation you give new sons and daughters to your Church, and we pray that *this child*, now to be received by Baptism, may know you better and love you more day by day, through Jesus Christ your Son our Lord. **Amen.**

The Ministry of the Word

4 An Old Testament Lesson or an Epistle may be read here.

5 A Sermon may be preached here.

6 These passages from the Gospels are read, or two of them may be read here and one later:

> The Gospel according to Mark, the first chapter, beginning at the ninth verse.

> In those days Jesus came from Nazareth of Galilee and was baptized by John in the Jordan. And when he came up out of the water, immediately he saw the heavens

opened and the Spirit descending upon him like a dove; and a voice came from heaven, 'Thou art my beloved Son; with thee I am well pleased.'

The Gospel according to Mark, the tenth chapter, beginning at the thirteenth verse.

They were bringing children to Jesus, that he might touch them: and the disciples rebuked them. But when Jesus saw it he was indignant, and said to them, 'Let the children come to me, do not hinder them; for to such belongs the kingdom of God. Truly, I say to you, whoever does not receive the kingdom of God like a child shall not enter it.' And he took them in his arms and blessed them, laying his hands upon them.

The Gospel according to Matthew, the twenty-eighth chapter, beginning at the eighteenth verse.

Jesus came and said to them, 'All authority in heaven and on earth has been given to me. Go therefore and make disciples of all nations, baptizing them in the name of the Father and of the Son and of the Holy Spirit, teaching them to observe all that I have commanded you; and lo, I am with you always, to the close of the age.'

7   The Minister says:

Thus the children of Christian parents are brought to be baptized with water as a sign of the new life in Christ, and to be made members of God's family the Church. We bring *this child* whom God has entrusted to us and claim for *him* all that Christ has won for us. Christ loves *him* and is ready to receive *him*, to embrace *him* with the arms of his mercy and to give *him* the blessing of eternal life.

A7

The Baptismal Prayer

8   The Minister at the Font and the people, all standing, say:

> **Father, we thank you that you have created all things and made us in your own image;**
> **That after we had fallen into sin you did not leave us in darkness, but sent your only Son Jesus Christ to be our Saviour;**
> **That by his death and resurrection he broke the power of evil;**
> **And that by sending the Holy Spirit you have made us a new creation.**

The Minister says:

> Father, be present with us in the power of your Spirit.
> We pray that *this child*, now to be baptized in this water, may die to sin and be raised to the new life in Christ. **Amen.**
> We pray that *he* may learn to trust Jesus Christ as *his* Lord and Saviour.   **Amen.**
> We pray that by the power of the Holy Spirit *he* may have victory over evil.   **Amen.**
> From darkness lead *him* to light, from death lead *him* to eternal life, through Jesus Christ our Lord.   **Amen.**

The Promises and the Profession of Faith

9   The Minister says to the congregation:

> Members of the Body of Christ, who are now in his name

to receive *this child*, will you so maintain the common life of worship and service that *he* and all the children among you may grow in grace and in the knowledge and love of God and of his Son Jesus Christ our Lord?

With God's help we will.

10   The Minister says to the parents or guardians of the *child*:

You have brought *this child* to be baptized, and you will receive *him* again to be trained in the doctrines, privileges and duties of the Christian religion. I ask you therefore:
Will you provide for *this your child* a Christian home of love and faithfulness?

Answer: With God's help we will.

Will you help *him* by your words, prayers and example to renounce all evil and to put *his* trust in Jesus Christ *his* Saviour?

Answer: With God's help we will.

Will you encourage *him* to enter into the full membership of the Church, and to serve Christ in the world?

Answer: With God's help we will.

11   If there are sponsors, the Minister says:

Will you, who have come to support these parents, help them in the Christian upbringing of *this child?*

Answer: With God's help we will.

12 The Minister says:

Let us confess the faith of the Church:

All say EITHER the Apostles' Creed:

I believe in God, the Father almighty,
creator of heaven and earth.

I believe in Jesus Christ, his only Son, our Lord.
He was conceived by the power of the Holy Spirit
and born of the Virgin Mary.
He suffered under Pontius Pilate,
was crucified, died, and was buried.
He descended to the dead.
On the third day he rose again.
He ascended into heaven,
and is seated at the right hand of the Father.
He will come again to judge the living and the dead.

I believe in the Holy Spirit,
the holy catholic Church,
the communion of saints,
the forgiveness of sins,
the resurrection of the body,
and the life everlasting.   Amen.

OR

We believe in God the Father,
who made the world;
And in his Son, Jesus Christ,
who redeemed mankind;
And in the Holy Spirit,
who sanctifies the People of God.   Amen.

13   Then the Minister says to the parents or guardians:

> Do you then present *this your child* to be baptized?

Answer: We do.

The Baptism

14   The Minister, taking each child into *his* arms, says to the parents or guardians: Name this child; and, naming *him* accordingly, pours or sprinkles water upon *him*, or dips *him* in water, saying: *N*., I baptize you in the Name of the Father, and of the Son, and of the Holy Spirit. **Amen.**

15   The Minister, making the sign of the cross on the forehead of the child, says:

> By Baptism we receive this child into the congregation of Christ's flock, and pray that *he* may not be ashamed to hold fast the faith of Christ crucified, to fight against evil, and to persevere as Christ's faithful soldier and servant to *his* life's end. **Amen.**

All say or sing:

> **The Lord bless you and keep you; the Lord make his face to shine upon you, and be gracious unto you; the Lord lift up his countenance upon you, and give you peace.**
> **Amen.**

17 The Minister, or the Baptismal Roll Secretary, may give to the parents or guardians of the *child* a lighted candle, saying to the *child*:

> I give you this sign, for you now belong to Christ, the light of the world.
> **Let your light so shine before men, that they may see your good works and give glory to your Father who is in heaven.**

The Final Prayers

18 EITHER the Minister says:

> Let us pray.
> Father, we thank you that you have received *this child* to be your own within your family the Church.
> May *he* grow in the faith in which *he* has been baptized and come to profess that faith before men. **Amen.**
> Bless the *home* of *this child* and give wisdom and affection to *his* parents that they may lead *him* in the way of perfect love. **Amen.**
> Strengthen your Church in the Holy Spirit that, through our worship and ministry to the world, *this child* may learn to follow Christ. **Amen.**

OR *he* prays in *his* own words.

19 The Minister, whether proceeding with the service of public
   worship or dismissing the people, says:

> The grace of the Lord Jesus Christ, and the love of God,
> and the fellowship of the Holy Spirit, be with us all.
> **Amen.**

20 At the main service of public worship further lessons are read
   and the sermon is preached if they have not come earlier; and
   the service then proceeds as it usually does after the sermon.
   The intercessions may be shortened or omitted, and the Creed
   is not said again.

Public Reception into Full Membership, or Confirmation

General Directions

1 Those who have by Baptism been admitted into the visible community of the Church are constantly to be taught to look forward to their reception into the full membership of the Church, when by professing their faith in Christ they will claim for themselves the promises of God, who by his Holy Spirit will strengthen them for his service.

2 When children sincerely desire to serve Jesus Christ, and are receiving regular instruction in the Bible and the Faith, their names shall be brought before the Pastoral sub-Committee. If they are approved, they shall be entered as 'Members in Training'. Before such children are admitted into full membership, the classes in which they have been meeting shall take the form of, or be supplemented by, a Preparation Class.

3 The names of candidates for full membership, other than children, shall similarly be brought before the Pastoral sub-Committee. If they are approved as Members in Training, the sub-Committee shall arrange for a Preparation Class.

4 In the Preparation Classes the Senior Catechism may be used.

5 All those who confess Jesus Christ as Lord and Saviour and accept the obligation to serve him in the life of the Church and the world are welcome as full members of the Methodist

Church. The Pastoral sub-Committee shall be satisfied of the sincerity of this desire as shown by evidence of life and conduct, by fidelity to the ordinances of the Church, and by the maintenance of Christian fellowship in the means of grace.

6 When those 'in Training' have thus been on probation for not less than three months, their names shall again be brought before the Pastoral sub-Committee, which, being thus satisfied, shall recommend such persons to the Church Council for admission into the membership of the Methodist Church. Those approved shall be admitted into full membership by the Church Council on that recommendation and be publicly recognized at the earliest opportunity at a service, to be known as the Service of Reception into Full Membership, or Confirmation, conducted by the Minister in the presence of the Church and including the Sacrament of the Lord's Supper. Such a service should be held at least once a year either for a local church or a group of local churches.

7 If any have not received Christian Baptism, that Sacrament should be administered either before or in connection with the Service of Public Reception into Full Membership or Confirmation. In this Service those who confess Jesus Christ as Lord and Saviour and accept the obligation to serve him in the life of the Church and the world, and who desire to have fellowship with the Methodist people, having been baptized and having been admitted into full membership by the Church Council, are publicly received into full membership, with all its duties and privileges, of the Methodist Church, which is within the Holy Catholic Church. As they commit themselves to Jesus Christ, their Lord and Saviour, prayer is made that the Holy Spirit, who alone makes them new creatures in him, may strengthen them by confirming the gifts which he has given.

The Service

This order is to be used when all those who are to be confirmed have already been baptized.

The Ministry of the Word

1   This or some other hymn may be sung:

> In the Name of Jesus
>   Every knee shall bow,
> Every tongue confess him
>   King of Glory now.
> 'Tis the Father's pleasure
>   We should call him Lord,
> Who from the beginning
>   Was the mighty Word.
>
> Humbled for a season,
>   To receive a name
> From the lips of sinners
>   Unto whom he came,
> Faithfully he bore it
>   Spotless to the last,
> Brought it back victorious
>   When from death he passed.

Name him, brothers, name him,
  With love strong as death,
But with awe and wonder,
  And with bated breath;
He is God the Saviour,
  He is Christ the Lord,
Ever to be worshipped,
  Trusted, and adored.

In your hearts enthrone him;
  There let him subdue
All that is not holy,
  All that is not true;
Crown him as your Captain
  In temptation's hour;
Let his will enfold you
  In its light and power.

Brothers, this Lord Jesus
  Shall return again
With his Father's glory,
  With his angel train;
For all wreaths of empire
  Meet upon his brow,
And our hearts confess him
  King of Glory now.

2   The Minister says this prayer, or prays in *his* own words:

Let us pray.

Heavenly Father, we thank you that by the preaching of the Gospel you have led *these* your *servants* to the knowledge of your truth; and we pray that the good work you have begun in *them* may be confirmed by the continued working of your Holy Spirit, through Jesus Christ our Lord.   **Amen.**

3   This or some other lesson from the Old Testament:

The Book of Jeremiah, the thirty-first chapter, beginning at the thirty-first verse.

Behold the days are coming, says the Lord, when I will make a new covenant with the house of Israel and the house of Judah, not like the covenant which I made with their fathers when I took them by the hand to bring them out of the land of Egypt, my covenant which they broke, though I was their husband, says the Lord. But this is the covenant which I will make with the house of Israel after those days, says the Lord: I will put my law within them, and I will write it upon their hearts; and I will be their God, and they shall be my people. And no longer shall each man teach his neighbour and each his brother, saying, 'Know the Lord', for they shall all know me, from the least of them to the greatest, says the Lord; for I will forgive their iniquity, and I will remember their sins no more.

4   This or some other Epistle:

The Letter of Paul to the Romans, the eighth chapter. beginning at the twelfth verse.

So then, brethren, we are debtors, not to the flesh, to live according to the flesh—for if you live according to the flesh you will die, but if by the Spirit you put to death the deeds of the body you will live. For all who are led by the Spirit of God are sons of God. For you did not receive the spirit of slavery to fall back into fear, but you have received the spirit of sonship. When we cry, 'Abba! Father!' it is the Spirit himself bearing witness with our spirit that we are children of God, and if children, then

heirs, heirs of God and fellow heirs with Christ, provided
we suffer with him in order that we may also be glorified
with him.

5   This or some other hymn may be sung:

> Christ, from whom all blessings flow,
> Perfecting the saints below,
> Hear us, who thy nature share,
> Who thy mystic body are.

> Join us, in one spirit join,
> Let us still receive of thine;
> Still for more on thee we call,
> Thou who fillest all in all.

> Move, and actuate, and guide:
> Divers gifts to each divide;
> Placed according to thy will,
> Let us all our work fulfil;

> Sweetly may we all agree,
> Touched with loving sympathy:
> Kindly for each other care;
> Every member feel its share.

> Love, like death, hath all destroyed,
> Rendered all distinctions void;
> Names, and sects, and parties fall;
> Thou, O Christ, art all in all.

6   The Gospel:

> The Gospel according to Mark, the first chapter, beginning at the fourteenth verse.

The people may say: **Glory to Christ our Saviour.**

> Now after John was arrested, Jesus came into Galilee, preaching the gospel of God, and saying, 'The time is fulfilled, and the kingdom of God is at hand; repent, and believe in the gospel.'
> And passing along by the Sea of Galilee, he saw Simon and Andrew the brother of Simon casting a net in the sea; for they were fishermen. And Jesus said to them, 'Follow me and I will make you become fishers of men.' And immediately they left their nets and followed him. And going on a little farther, he saw James the son of Zebedee and John his brother, who were in the boat mending the nets. And immediately he called them; and they left their father Zebedee in the boat with the hired servants, and followed him.

The people may say: **Praise to Christ our Lord.**

7   The Sermon

8   This or some other hymn may be sung:

> **O thou who camest from above**
> **The pure celestial fire to impart,**
> **Kindle a flame of sacred love**
> **On the mean altar of my heart!**

There let it for thy glory burn
    With inextinguishable blaze:
And trembling to its source return,
    In humble prayer and fervent praise.

Jesus, confirm my heart's desire
    To work, and speak, and think for thee;
Still let me guard the holy fire,
    And still stir up thy gift in me.

Ready for all thy perfect will,
    My acts of faith and love repeat,
Till death thy endless mercies seal,
    And make the sacrifice complete.   Amen.

9   Those who are to be confirmed stand, and the Minister says to them:

Beloved in Christ, at your Baptism you were received into God's family the Church. You have grown in the knowledge and love of our Lord. You have heard Christ saying to you, as he said to his first disciples, Follow me. You have already responded to his call, and you come now by your own choice publicly to renounce evil and profess your faith in him. You are now to be confirmed as *members* of a chosen race, a royal priesthood, a holy nation, God's own people, sent forth as Christ's *servants* and *witnesses* into the world. For all this God will strengthen you by his Holy Spirit.

The Promises and the Profession of Faith

10 The Minister asks these questions, and those who are to be confirmed answer, the people also standing:

> I ask you therefore:
> Do you repent of your sins and renounce all evil?

Answer: I do.

> Do you trust in Jesus Christ as your Lord and Saviour?

Answer: I do.

> Will you obey Christ and serve him in the Church and in the world?

Answer: With his help I will.

11 The Minister says:

> Let us profess together the faith of the Church:

The Apostles' Creed

**I believe in God, the Father almighty,
creator of heaven and earth.**

**I believe in Jesus Christ, his only Son, our Lord.
He was conceived by the power of the Holy Spirit
and born of the Virgin Mary.
He suffered under Pontius Pilate,
was crucified, died, and was buried.**

He descended to the dead.
On the third day he rose again.
He ascended into heaven,
and is seated on the right hand of the Father.
He will come again to judge the living and the dead.

I believe in the Holy Spirit,
the holy catholic Church,
the communion of saints,
the forgiveness of sins,
the resurrection of the body,
and the life everlasting.   Amen.

The Confirmation and Reception

12   Those who are to be confirmed kneel, but the people remain standing, and the Minister says:

Heavenly Father, all-powerful God, who in Baptism received *these* your *children* into your family, establish *them* now in faith by the Holy Spirit, and day by day increase in *them* your gifts of grace;
the spirit of wisdom and understanding;   **Amen.**
the spirit of counsel and might;   **Amen.**
the spirit of knowledge and true godliness and the fear of the Lord;   **Amen.**
and keep *them* in your mercy for ever.   **Amen.**

13   EITHER

The Minister lays *his* hands upon the head of each one of them, saying:

Lord, confirm your servant *N.* by your Holy Spirit that *he* may continue to be yours for ever.
And each answers: Amen.

All stand, and the Minister says to those who have been confirmed:

> We welcome you into the full membership of the Christian Church and the Society in this place (*or*, the Societies of this Circuit).

The Minister and another representative member of the Society may give the right hand of fellowship to each of them.

OR
The Minister says:

> Lord, confirm *these* your *servants* by your Holy Spirit that *they* may continue to be yours for ever. **Amen.**

All stand, and the Minister welcomes each one severally, giving the right hand of fellowship, and saying:

> *N.*, we welcome you into the full membership of the Christian Church and the Society in this place (*or*, the Societies of this Circuit).

Another representative member of the Society may give the right hand of fellowship to each of them.

---

14 A Bible or some other book may be given here.

15 Then the Minister and the people, standing, say together:

> **Lord God, holy Father, we are not our own but yours. As you sent your Son into the world to save the world, so send us to serve our neighbours and to bring them to believe in him. Amen.**

16 The Lord's Prayer

>**Our Father . . .**

17 Hymn

>**Lord, in the strength of grace,**
>>**With a glad heart and free,**
>
>**Myself, my residue of days,**
>>**I consecrate to thee.**
>
>**Thy ransomed servant, I**
>>**Restore to thee thy own;**
>
>**And, from this moment, live or die**
>>**To serve my God alone.**

The Lord's Supper

18 The Minister proceeds to the Lord's Supper, beginning at the
Setting of the Table. For the hymn at no. 30 in *The Sunday
Service* this or some other hymn may be sung:

>**Ye servants of God,**
>>**Your Master proclaim,**
>
>**And publish abroad**
>>**His wonderful name;**
>
>**The name all-victorious**
>>**Of Jesus extol;**
>
>**His kingdom is glorious,**
>>**And rules over all.**

God ruleth on high,
   Almighty to save;
And still he is nigh,
   His presence we have;
The great congregation
   His triumph shall sing,
Ascribing salvation
   To Jesus our King.

Salvation to God
   Who sits on the throne!
Let all cry aloud,
   And honour the Son:
The praises of Jesus
   The angels proclaim,
Fall down on their faces,
   And worship the Lamb.

Then let us adore,
   And give him his right,
All glory and power,
   All wisdom and might,
All honour and blessing,
   With angels above,
And thanks never-ceasing,
   And infinite love.

19 If this service is used on Christmas Day, Easter Day, Ascension
    Day, Pentecost, or Trinity Sunday, then the Collect and Lessons
    of the Day are read in place of those given in this order of
    service.

The Baptism of those who are able to answer for themselves, with the Public Reception into Full Membership, or Confirmation

General Directions

1   Those who are able to answer for themselves, if they have not already received Christian Baptism, should first be instructed. The Senior Catechism may be used for this purpose. When the Minister is satisfied as to their repentance, faith, and desire for Baptism, he shall proceed to baptize them, preferably at a service of public worship. Two sponsors may be appointed by the Minister, in consultation with the candidate, to assist the candidate in carrying out his promise.

2   When those who are able to answer for themselves are baptized together with their children, the order for the Baptism of those who are able to answer for themselves shall be used, with such additions as are necessary; and after the parents have made their own promises they shall make those that relate to the upbringing of their children.

3   If an unbaptized person who is of age to answer for *himself* is dying and desires to be baptized, the Minister, if he is satisfied as to *his* repentance, faith and desire for Baptism, may baptize *him* in the same way in which infants are baptized in an emergency; and if *he* recovers *he* may come to the church in order that the congregation may publicly welcome *him*; and *he* should be further instructed in order that *he* may be received as a full member as soon as possible.

4   Those who are to be baptized when they are able to answer for themselves will normally have fulfilled the requirements for full membership, and been admitted accordingly by the Church Council. Thus, when they are baptized, they shall normally proceed at once to the Public Reception into Full Membership, or Confirmation. Therefore, the order of service for their Baptism includes also their Public Reception, or Confirmation; nevertheless for good reason this service may be used without Public Reception or Confirmation, which should then follow after an interval of time.

5   If at a service for Public Reception, or Confirmation, some have already been baptized and others have not, then the order of service for the Baptism of those who are able to answer for themselves with Public Reception into Full Membership, or Confirmation, shall be used.

6   The Baptism of those who are able to answer for themselves takes place normally at a public service, but for pastoral reasons it may take place at some other occasion. If so, immediately after the Baptism the service concludes with the Final Prayers or with a blessing only, and some time later the Service of Public Reception into Full Membership, or Confirmation, takes place.

7   The General Directions for Public Reception into Full Membership or Confirmation (p. 14) should also be consulted.

A28

The Service

The Ministry of the Word

1   This or some other hymn may be sung:

Being of beings, God of love,
    To thee our hearts we raise:
Thy all-sustaining power we prove,
    And gladly sing thy praise.

Thine, wholly thine, we long to be;
    Our sacrifice receive:
Made, and preserved, and saved by thee,
    To thee ourselves we give.

Heavenward our every wish aspires;
    For all thy mercies' store
The sole return thy love requires
    Is that we ask for more.

For more we ask; we open then
    Our hearts to embrace thy will;
Turn, and revive us, Lord, again,
    With all thy fullness fill.

Come, Holy Ghost, the Saviour's love
    Shed in our hearts abroad;
So shall we ever live, and move,
    And be with Christ in God.

2   The Minister says this prayer or prays in *his* own words:

> Let us pray.
>
> Heavenly Father, who gave us the Sacrament of Holy Baptism, we pray that *these* your *servants* may be made members of the Body of your Son by Baptism and so share his death and resurrection, through the same Jesus Christ our Lord. **Amen.**

3   This or some other lesson from the Old Testament:

> The Book of Ezekiel, the thirty-sixth chapter, beginning at the twenty-fifth verse.
>
> I will sprinkle clean water upon you, and you shall be clean from all your uncleannesses, and from all your idols I will cleanse you. A new heart I will give you, and a new spirit I will put within you; and I will take out of your flesh the heart of stone and give you a heart of flesh. And I will put my spirit within you, and cause you to walk in my statutes and be careful to observe my ordinances. You shall dwell in the land which I gave to your fathers; and you shall be my people, and I will be your God.

4   This or some other Epistle:

> The Letter of Paul to the Romans, the sixth chapter, beginning at the third verse.
>
> Do you not know that all of us who have been baptized into Christ Jesus were baptized into his death? We were buried therefore with him by baptism into death, so that as Christ was raised from the dead by the glory of the Father, we too might walk in newness of life.

For if we have been united with him in a death like his, we shall certainly be united with him in a resurrection like his. We know that our old self was crucified with him so that the sinful body might be destroyed, and we might no longer be enslaved in sin. For he who has died is freed from sin. But if we have died with Christ, we believe that we shall also live with him. For we know that Christ being raised from the dead will never die again; death no longer has dominion over him. The death he died he died to sin, once for all, but the life he lives he lives to God. So you must consider yourselves dead to sin and alive to God in Christ Jesus.

5   This or some other hymn may be sung:

Come, Father, Son, and Holy Ghost,
   Honour the means ordained by thee;
Make good our apostolic boast,
   And own thy glorious ministry.

We now thy promised presence claim;
   Sent to disciple all mankind,
Sent to baptize into thy name,
   We now thy promised presence find.

Father, in these reveal thy Son;
   In these, for whom we seek thy face,
The hidden mystery make known,
   The inward, pure, baptizing grace.

Jesus, with us thou always art;
   Effectual make the sacred sign,
The gift unspeakable impart,
   And bless the ordinance divine.

Eternal Spirit, descend from high,
    Baptizer of our spirits thou!
The sacramental seal apply,
    And witness with the water now.

O that the souls baptized therein
    May now thy truth and mercy feel;
May rise and wash away their sin;
    Come, Holy Ghost, their pardon seal.

6   This Gospel:

The Gospel according to John, the third chapter, beginning at the first verse.

The people may say: **Glory to Christ our Saviour.**

Now there was a man of the Pharisees, named Nicodemus, a ruler of the Jews. This man came to Jesus by night and said to him, 'Rabbi, we know that you are a teacher come from God; for no one can do these signs that you do, unless God is with him.' Jesus answered him, 'Truly, truly, I say to you, unless one is born anew, he cannot see the kingdom of God.' Nicodemus said to him, 'How can a man be born when he is old? Can he enter a second time into his mother's womb and be born?' Jesus answered, 'Truly, truly, I say to you, unless one is born of water and the spirit, he cannot enter the kingdom of God. That which is born of the Spirit is spirit. Do not marvel that I said to you, "You must be born anew".'

The people may say: **Praise to Christ our Lord.**

7   The Sermon

8   This or some other hymn may be sung:

> O thou who camest from above
>   The pure celestial fire to impart,
> Kindle a flame of sacred love
>   On the mean altar of my heart!
>
> There let it for thy glory burn
>   With inextinguishable blaze;
> And trembling to its source return,
>   In humble prayer and fervent praise.
>
> Jesus, confirm my heart's desire
>   To work, and speak, and think for thee;
> Still let me guard the holy fire,
>   And still stir up thy gift in me.
>
> Ready for all thy perfect will,
>   My acts of faith and love repeat,
> Till death thy endless mercies seal,
>   And make the sacrifice complete.   Amen.

9   The Minister and those who are to be baptized, with their sponsors, come to the Font; and the Minister says:

> Beloved in Christ, we learn from the Gospels that our
> Lord Jesus Christ, when he was baptized in the River
> Jordan, received the Holy Spirit. He taught us that we
> must be born again if we are to enter the kingdom of
> God. He died and rose again for our sins, and com-
> manded his Church to make disciples of all the nations,
> baptizing them in the Name of the Father, and of the
> Son, and of the Holy Spirit. He has poured out this
> Spirit upon his Church, and those who are baptized into
> him share his death and resurrection.

Thus we know that God will receive *these persons* who *turn* to him in repentance and faith, and will forgive *their* sins. He will bestow on *them* new life through the Holy Spirit and make *them* members of his Church.

The Baptismal Prayer

10 The Minister at the Font and the people, all standing, say:

Holy Father, Lord of all power, ever-living God, we proclaim your glory. You have created all things and made us in your own image. After we had fallen into sin, you did not leave us in darkness, but sent your only Son, Jesus Christ, to be our Saviour.

We thank you that he took our nature upon him, that he was baptized in Jordan and anointed with the Holy Spirit, and went about doing good, that he died on the cross and rose again for our salvation, and that after his ascension he poured forth his Holy Spirit upon his people to make of them a new creation.

The Minister says:

Father, be present with us in the power of your Spirit to fulfil your promises:

We pray that *they* who *are* now to be baptized in this water, having professed *their* faith in Christ, and being born again of the Spirit, may die to sin and be raised to the new life of righteousness in Christ. **Amen.**

We pray that, being baptized into Christ's Body the Church by the power of the Spirit, *they* may have victory over evil. **Amen.**

From darkness lead *them* to light, from death lead *them* to eternal life, through Jesus Christ our Lord.   **Amen.**

The Promises and the Profession of Faith

11   The Minister says to the people:

> Members of the Body of Christ, who are now in Christ's name to receive *these persons*, will you so maintain the common life of worship and service that *they* may grow in grace and in the knowledge and love of God and of his Son Jesus Christ our Lord?

With God's help we will.

12   The Minister speaks to those who are to be baptized, and also to any who, having already been baptized, are now to be confirmed; and they all answer.

> You have heard Jesus saying to you, as he said to his first disciples, Follow me. You have already responded to his call, and you sincerely desire to be saved from your sins through faith in him. I ask you therefore: Do you repent of your sins and renounce all evil?

Answer: I do.

> Do you trust in Jesus Christ as your Lord and Saviour?

Answer: I do.

Will you obey Christ and serve him in the Church and in the world?

Answer: With his help I will.

13 The Minister says:

Let us profess together the faith of the Church.

The Apostles' Creed

I believe in God, the Father almighty,
creator of heaven and earth.

I believe in Jesus Christ, his only Son, our Lord.
He was conceived by the power of the Holy Spirit
and born of the Virgin Mary.
He suffered under Pontius Pilate,
was crucified, died, and was buried.
He descended to the dead.
On the third day he rose again.
He ascended into heaven,
and is seated at the right hand of the Father.
He will come again to judge the living and the dead.

I believe in the Holy Spirit,
the holy catholic Church,
the communion of saints,
the forgiveness of sins,
the resurrection of the body,
and the life everlasting.   Amen.

14 The Minister says to those who are to be baptized:

Do you then wish to be baptized?

Answer: I do.

The Baptism

15 The Minister asks the sponsors or other witnesses to give the Christian name or names of each person to be baptized, and then, naming the person accordingly, pours or sprinkles water upon *him*, or dips *him* in water, saying:

> *N.*, I baptize you in the Name of the Father, and of the Son, and of the Holy Spirit.   **Amen.**

The Confirmation and Reception

16 Those who are baptized when they are able to answer for themselves normally proceed at once to Confirmation; but if the Confirmation be delayed or there be no Confirmation, then that which follows is omitted, and the Minister proceeds to page 41.

17 When there are others to be confirmed who have been baptized previously, the Minister says to them:

> Beloved in Christ, at your Baptism you were received into God's family the Church. You have grown in the knowledge and love of our Lord. You have heard Christ saying to you, as he said to his first disciples, Follow me. You have already responded to his call and have by your own choice publicly renounced evil and professed your faith in him. You are now to be confirmed as *members* of a chosen race, a royal priesthood, a holy nation, God's own people, sent forth as Christ's *servants* and *witnesses* into the world. For all this God will strengthen you by his Holy Spirit.

18 Those who are to be confirmed kneel, but the people remain standing, and the Minister says:

> Heavenly Father, all-powerful God, who in Baptism received *these* your *children* into your family, establish *them* now in faith by the Holy Spirit, and day by day increase in *them* your gifts of grace;
> the spirit of wisdom and understanding; **Amen.**
> the spirit of counsel and might; **Amen.**
> the spirit of knowledge and true godliness and the fear of the Lord; **Amen.**
> and keep *them* in your mercy for ever. **Amen.**

19 EITHER

The Minister lays *his* hand upon the head of each one of them, saying:

> Lord, confirm your servant *N.* by your Holy Spirit that *he* may continue to be yours for ever.

And each answers: Amen.

All stand, and the Minister says to those who have been confirmed:

> We welcome you into the full membership of the Christian Church and the Society in this place (*or*, the Societies of this Circuit).

The Minister and another representative member of the Society may give the right hand of fellowship to each of them.

OR

The Minister says:

> Lord, confirm *these* your *servants* by your Holy Spirit that *they* may continue to be yours for ever. **Amen.**

All stand, and the Minister welcomes each one severally, giving the right hand of fellowship, and saying:

> *N.*, we welcome you into the full membership of the Christian Church and the Society in this place (*or*, the Societies of this Circuit).

Another representative member of the Society may give the right hand of fellowship to each of them.

20 A Bible or some other book may be given here.

21 Then the Minister and the people, standing, say together:

> **Lord God, holy Father, we are not our own but yours. As you sent your Son into the world to save the world, so send us to serve our neighbours and to bring them to believe in him. Amen.**

22 The Lord's Prayer

> **Our Father . . .**

> Lord, in the strength of grace,
>   With a glad heart and free,
> Myself, my residue of days,
>   I consecrate to thee.
>
> Thy ransomed servant, I
>   Restore to thee thy own;
> And, from this moment, live or die
>   To serve my God alone.

The Lord's Supper

24 The Minister proceeds to the Lord's Supper, beginning at the Setting of the Table. For the hymn at no. 30 in *The Sunday Service* this or some other hymn may be sung:

> Now thank we all our God,
>   With hearts, and hands, and voices;
> Who wondrous things hath done,
>   In whom his world rejoices;
> Who, from our mothers' arms,
>   Hath blessed us on our way
> With countless gifts of love,
>   And still is ours today.
>
> O may this bounteous God
>   Through all our life be near us,
> With ever joyful hearts
>   And blessèd peace to cheer us,

And keep us in his grace,
    And guide us when perplexed,
And free us from all ills
    In this world and the next.

All praise and thanks to God
    The Father now be given,
The Son, and him who reigns
    With them in highest heaven:
The one, eternal God,
    Whom earth and heaven adore;
For thus it was, is now,
    And shall be evermore.   Amen.

If this service is used on Christmas Day, Easter Day, Ascension Day, Pentecost, or Trinity Sunday, then the Collect and Lessons of the Day are read in the place of those given in this order of service.

Appendix A

These prayers may be used if, in exceptional circumstances and for good reason, Confirmation does not immediately follow the Baptism of those who are able to answer for themselves.

The Minister, making the sign of the cross on the forehead of each person, says:

By Baptism we receive *this person* into the congregation of Christ's flock, and pray that *he* may not be ashamed to hold fast the faith of Christ crucified, to fight against evil, and to persevere as Christ's faithful soldier and servant to *his* life's end.   **Amen.**

All say or sing:

> **The Lord bless you and keep you; the Lord make his face to shine upon you, and be gracious unto you; the Lord lift up his countenance upon you, and give you peace.**
>
> **Amen.**

The Minister says this prayer or prays in *his* own words:

> Let us pray.
>
> Father, we thank you that you have received *these* your *servants* to be your own within your family the Church. Continue the work you have begun in *them* that *they* may bear witness to your love for all the world.   **Amen.**

The Minister, whether proceeding with the service of public worship or dismissing the people, says:

> The grace of the Lord Jesus Christ, and the love of God, and the fellowship of the Holy Spirit, be with us all.
>
> **Amen.**

Appendix B*

1   Persons being received from other Christian communions, if they have not been previously baptized, should be baptized.

---

*These directions were given by Conference 1970, but 'Leaders' Meeting' has been altered to 'Church Council'.

2 If they have not been confirmed or full members of another Christian communion and now wish to be full members of the Methodist Church, they should be confirmed and received into full membership.

3 If they have already been confirmed or full members of another Christian communion from which they can be received by transfer, they should be received into full membership of the Methodist Church by being admitted into membership of a local society without any public service, like members being received by transfer from another Methodist society.

4 If they are confirmed or full members of another Christian communion from which they cannot be received by transfer, then the Minister shall ascertain that, after due consideration of the teaching and practice of the Methodist Church, they desire to take up its duties and privileges, and the Church Council shall admit them into full membership; and then, if pastoral reasons so require, they may be publicly received in this way, preferably after the Sermon, at a service which is to include the Lord's Supper.

The Minister says:

> N., you have been a member of another communion within the Church of Christ. Do you, having duly considered the teaching and practice of the Methodist Church, desire to take up the duties and privileges of membership?

Answer: I do.

The Minister gives to *him* the right hand of fellowship, saying:

> *N.*, we welcome you into the full membership of the Methodist Church and the Society in this place.

Prayer is offered for the person newly received, and afterwards *he* receives the Holy Communion.

Another version of The Apostles' Creed

I believe in God the Father Almighty,
maker of heaven and earth:

And in Jesus Christ his only Son our Lord,
who was conceived by the Holy Ghost,
born of the Virgin Mary,
suffered under Pontius Pilate,
was crucified, dead, and buried,
he descended into hell;
the third day he rose again from the dead,
he ascended into heaven,
and sitteth on the right hand of God the Father Almighty;
from thence he shall come
to judge the quick and the dead.

I believe in the Holy Ghost;
the holy Catholic Church;
the Communion of Saints;
the Forgiveness of sins;
the Resurrection of the body;
and the Life everlasting.   Amen.

The Sunday Service

General Directions

1 The worship of the Church is the offering of praise and prayer in which God's Word is read and preached, and in its fullness it includes the Lord's Supper, or Holy Communion.

2 It is the privilege and duty of members of the Methodist Church to avail themselves of this Sacrament. Communicant members of other Churches whose discipline so permits are also welcome to receive it.

3 The first of the following orders of service consists of the Preparation and the Ministry of the Word, leading into the Lord's Supper. There is also provided a Service for use when there is no Communion.

4 The basic elements are marked by the symbol ▶, and the other sections may be omitted. The Commandments of the Lord Jesus and the Ten Commandments are appropriately read on the first or another Sunday in Advent and Lent respectively.

5 Whenever the Lord's Supper is observed, God's Word should first be read and, however briefly, should be expounded.

6 *The Sunday Service* may be used on other special days and occasions.

7 At the Lord's Supper an ordained Minister, or a person with a dispensation for the purpose, shall preside. Laymen may be invited to share in the Preparation; the Ministry of the Word,

including the intercessions; and in the distribution of the bread and wine.

8   The Preparation may sometimes be confined to the opening hymn and the collect of the day. At Easter, for instance, a penitential introduction is not appropriate. Usually, however, numbers 4 and 5 should not be omitted. Numbers 6 and 7 may be transposed, and this is especially appropriate when 7 takes the form of 'Glory to God in the highest'.

9   The place of Baptism and ordinances such as Confirmation is indicated in those Services. Acts of dedication and commissioning should normally follow the sermon.

10   In place of the Confession provided, the Minister may use *his* own words or read some other prayer. In place of a hymn, a psalm, or portion of a psalm, or canticle may be sung or said.

11   If an alternative to the declaration of forgiveness is required, it should be in the words of Scripture. One or other of the 'Comfortable Words', Matt. 11:28; John 3:16; 1 Tim. 1:15; 1 John 2:1-2, may be read.

12   For the lessons reference should be made to *Collects, Lessons and Psalms*.

13   When the Lord's Supper is being observed, it is fitting to stand for the Gospel.

14   If children are to leave for their own sessions, they may do so either after the Preparation or after the readings from Scripture are finished. They may have their own closing worship or return to the congregation.

15   Announcements may be made before the first hymn, or before the collect of the day, or before the intercessions, or after the Lord's Prayer.

16 There should normally be only one collection of money during the Service. When there is Communion, the collection may be taken as the congregation enters, or before the intercessions, or before the Setting of the Table. Preferably it should be presented at the Setting of the Table, but it may be presented at other times. Provision should be made from it for those in need. If for good reason there are to be two collections, one of them should be taken as the congregation enters or leaves. When there is no Communion, the collection may be taken as the congregation enters, or before the intercessions or before the prayer of thanksgiving and dedication.

17 In addition to the prescribed periods of silence there may be others, e.g. before the confession, before the intercessions, and after each petition of the intercessions.

18 The Peace may be given throughout the congregation by a handclasp from one member to another.

19 The Nicene Creed is traditionally used at the Eucharist, but for good reason the Apostles' Creed may be said as an alternative. The Creed may, if desired, be said after the Sermon instead of in the place provided.

20 The juice of the grape shall be used.

21 The prayer of humble access (no. 24) may be said by all the people, or by the Minister alone.

22 In the prayer of thanksgiving (no. 21) after the words 'celebrate your mighty acts' special thanksgivings may be inserted.

23 At every celebration the worshippers present should communicate unless there is good reason to the contrary. Children may be given a blessing at the Communion rail.

24 At the end of the Service, what remains of the elements should be disposed of reverently.

The Service

The Preparation

1 Hymn

2   Almighty God,
      to whom all hearts are open,
      all desires known,
      and from whom no secrets are hid:
      cleanse the thoughts of our hearts
      by the inspiration of your Holy Spirit,
      that we may perfectly love you,
      and worthily magnify your holy Name;
      through Christ our Lord. **Amen.**

3 The Commandments, when they are to be read (see pp.22-3)

4   Let us confess our sins to God.

      Almighty God, our heavenly Father,
      we have sinned against you and against our fellow men,
      in thought and word and deed,
      in the evil we have done
      and in the good we have not done,
      through ignorance, through weakness,
      through our own deliberate fault.
      We are truly sorry and repent of all our sins.
      For the sake of your Son, Jesus Christ, who died for us,
      forgive us all that is past;
      and grant that we may serve you in newness of life
      to the glory of your Name. Amen.

5   Christ Jesus came into the world to save sinners.

Hear then the word of grace:
Your sins are forgiven.

Amen. Thanks be to God.

▶ 6 **The Collect** of the Day, or some other prayer

7 Hymn, or **Glory to God in the highest**

**Glory to God in the highest,
And peace to his people on earth.**

**Lord God, heavenly King,
almighty God and Father,
we worship you, we give you thanks,
we praise you for your glory.**

**Lord Jesus Christ, only Son of the Father,
Lord God, Lamb of God,
you take away the sin of the world:
have mercy on us;
you are seated at the right hand of the Father:
receive our prayer.**

**For you alone are the Holy One,
you alone are the Lord,
you alone are the Most High,
Jesus Christ, with the Holy Spirit,
in the glory of God the Father.   Amen.**

The Ministry of the Word

▶ 8   The Old Testament Lesson, or the Epistle, or both

9   Hymn

10   When the Gospel has been announced the people may say:

Glory to Christ our Saviour.

▶   The Gospel

After the Gospel the people may say:

Praise to Christ our Lord.

▶ 11   The Sermon

▶ 12   The Intercessions (for other possible forms see pp.24-31)

Let us pray.

God, our Father, grant us the help of your Spirit in our prayers for the salvation of mankind.

We pray for the Church throughout the world [for . . .] and for this church and all its members [for . . .] that in faith and unity we may be constantly renewed by your Holy Spirit for mission and service.

Lord, in your mercy
Hear our prayer.

We pray for the peoples of the world and their leaders [for . . .] that they may seek justice, freedom and peace for all men.

Lord, in your mercy
Hear our prayer.

We pray for our own country and for all who have authority and influence [for . . .] that they may serve their fellows in wisdom, honesty and compassion.

Lord, in your mercy
Hear our prayer.

We pray for those among whom we live and work [for . . .] that we may rightly use your gifts to set men free from drudgery and want and together find joy in your creation.

Lord, in your mercy
Hear our prayer.

We pray for all in sorrow, need, anxiety and sickness [for . . .] for the lonely and the persecuted [for . . .] and for all who suffer from cruelty, injustice and neglect [for . . .] that in their weakness they may know your strength, and in despair find hope.

Lord, in your mercy
Hear our prayer.

In you, Father, we are one family in earth and heaven. We remember in your presence those who have died . . . giving thanks especially for those who have revealed to us your grace in Christ. Help us to follow the example of your saints in light and bring us with them into the fullness of your eternal joy, through Jesus Christ our Lord. **Amen.**

▶ 13   The Lord's Prayer

Our Father . . .

14   Those who leave do so now, after this blessing:

The grace of the Lord Jesus be with you all.   Amen.

The Lord's Supper

▶15 The Peace

> The peace of the Lord be always with you.
>
> **And also with you.**

16 The Peace may be given throughout the congregation with the words:

> **The peace of the Lord.**

17 The Nicene Creed

> **We believe in one God,**
> **the Father, the Almighty,**
> **maker of heaven and earth,**
> **of all that is, seen and unseen.**
>
> **We believe in one Lord, Jesus Christ,**
> **the only Son of God,**
> **eternally begotten of the Father,**
> **God from God, Light from Light,**
> **true God from true God,**
> **begotten, not made,**
> **of one Being with the Father.**
> **Through him all things were made.**
> **For us men and for our salvation**
> **he came down from heaven:**
> **by the power of the Holy Spirit**
> **he became incarnate from the Virgin Mary, and was**
> **   made man.**

For our sake he was crucified under Pontius Pilate;
he suffered death and was buried.
On the third day he rose again
in accordance with the Scriptures;
he ascended into heaven
and is seated at the right hand of the Father.
He will come again in glory
to judge the living and the dead,
and his kingdom will have no end.

We believe in the Holy Spirit, the Lord, the giver of life,
who proceeds from the Father and the Son.
With the Father and the Son he is worshipped and glorified.
He has spoken through the Prophets.
We believe in one holy catholic and apostolic Church.
We acknowledge one baptism for the forgiveness of sins.
We look for the resurrection of the dead,
and the life of the world to come.   Amen.

THE SETTING OF THE TABLE

18 Hymn

▶19 Bread and wine are brought to the Minister, or, being already on the table, are uncovered.

▶20 The Minister takes the bread and wine and prepares them for use.

THE THANKSGIVING

▶21 All stand.

The Minister says the great prayer of thanksgiving:

Lift up your hearts.

We lift them to the Lord.

Let us give thanks to the Lord our God.

It is right to give him thanks and praise.

Father, all-powerful and ever-living God,
it is indeed right, it is our joy and our salvation,
always and everywhere to give you thanks and praise
through Jesus Christ your Son our Lord.
You created all things and made us in your own image.
When we had fallen into sin, you gave your only Son to
be our Saviour.

He shared our human nature, and died on the cross.
You raised him from the dead, and exalted him to your
right hand in glory, where he lives for ever to pray for us.
Through him you have sent your holy and life-giving
Spirit and made us your people, a royal priesthood,
to stand before you to proclaim your glory and
celebrate your mighty acts.
And so with all the company of heaven we join in
the unending hymn of praise:

Holy, holy, holy Lord,
God of power and might,
heaven and earth are full of your glory.
Hosanna in the highest.
Blessed is he who comes in the name of the Lord.
Hosanna in the highest.

We praise you, Lord God, King of the universe,
through our Lord Jesus Christ,
who, on the night in which he was betrayed,
took bread, gave thanks, broke it, and gave it to his
disciples, saying,
'Take this and eat it. This is my body given for you.
Do this in remembrance of me.'
In the same way, after supper,
he took the cup, gave thanks, and gave it to them, saying,
'Drink from it all of you.
This is my blood of the new covenant,
poured out for you and for many, for the forgiveness
of sins.
Do this, whenever you drink it, in remembrance of me.'

Christ has died.
Christ is risen.
Christ will come again.

Therefore, Father, as he has commanded us,
we do this in remembrance of him,
and we ask you to accept our sacrifice of praise and
thanksgiving.

Grant that by the power of the Holy Spirit
we who receive your gifts of bread and wine
may share in the body and blood of Christ.

Make us one body with him.

Accept us as we offer ourselves to be a living sacrifice,
and bring us with the whole creation to your
heavenly kingdom.

We ask this through your Son, Jesus Christ our Lord.

Through him, with him, in him,
in the unity of the Holy Spirit,
all honour and glory be given to you, almighty Father,
from all who dwell on earth and in heaven
throughout all ages.   Amen.

THE BREAKING OF THE BREAD

▶ 22   The Minister breaks the bread in the sight of the people, in
silence, or saying,

EITHER :

The bread we break is a sharing in the body of Christ.

Though we are many, we are one body
because we all share in the one loaf.

OR:

> The things of God for God's holy people.

> **Jesus Christ is holy, Jesus Christ is Lord
> to the glory of God the Father.**

OR, from Easter Day to Pentecost:

> Alleluia, Christ our Passover is sacrificed for us.

> **Therefore let us keep the feast. Alleluia.**

▶ 23   Silence, all seated or kneeling

THE SHARING OF THE BREAD AND WINE

24
> Lord, we come to your table trusting in your mercy
> and not in any goodness of our own.
> We are not worthy even to gather up the crumbs under
> your table, but it is your nature always to have mercy,
> and on that we depend.
> So feed us with the body and blood of Jesus Christ,
> your Son, that we may for ever live in him and he in us.
>   **Amen.**

▶ 25   The Minister and any who are assisting *him* receive the bread
and wine and then give them to the people.

The Minister may say these or other words of invitation:

> Draw near with faith. Receive the body of our Lord
> Jesus Christ, which was given for you, and his blood,
> which was shed for you; and feed on him in your
> hearts by faith with thanksgiving.

▶26   **The bread** and wine are given EITHER with these words:

> The body of Christ given for you.

> The blood of Christ shed for you.

OR with these words:

> The body of our Lord Jesus Christ, which was given for you, keep you in eternal life. Take and eat this in remembrance that Christ died for you, and feed on him in your heart by faith with thanksgiving.

> The blood of our Lord Jesus Christ, which was shed for you, keep you in eternal life. Drink this in remembrance that Christ's blood was shed for you, and be thankful.

The communicant may reply each time: Amen.

▶27   **The Minister** covers what remains of the elements with a white cloth.

THE FINAL PRAYERS

▶ 28 Silence

▶ 29   Let us pray.

         **We thank you, Lord,
         that you have fed us in this sacrament,
         united us with Christ,
         and given us a foretaste of the heavenly banquet
         prepared for all mankind.   Amen.**

  30 Hymn

  31   The blessing of God, Father, Son, and Holy Spirit,
         remain with you always.   **Amen.**

▶ 32   Go in peace in the power of the Spirit
         to live and work to God's praise and glory.

         Thanks be to God.

The Sunday Service without the Lord's Supper

In many churches of the Reformation tradition it has been the custom, once on a Sunday, for the shape of the service to reflect that of the complete order of Word and Sacrament even when there is no celebration of the Lord's Supper, and the outline that follows is offered as a guide for this purpose. Other outlines may be used for a second service.

This outline consists of three principal parts: The Preparation, including praise and penitence; the Ministry of the Word; the Response. Hymns should be inserted at appropriate points, as should the notices and the collection. Prayer may be offered extempore in any place where prayer is suggested.

The Preparation
Prayers of adoration (unless this theme has been sufficiently expressed in a hymn) and confession, with an assurance of God's forgiveness.

The Ministry of the Word
Readings of Scripture, normally not less than two. The lectionary offers a selection including Old Testament, Epistle and Gospel, linked by a unifying theme; its use is strongly commended.
The sermon should be so placed as to make clear its link with the Scriptures from which it arises.
One or other of the historic creeds might well be used in this part of the service.

The Response

Thanksgiving and Intercession in whichever order is thought fitting, concluding with Dedication of ourselves, and the Lord's Prayer. Principal subjects for a prayer of thanksgiving should be: God's work in creation; the revelation of himself to men; the salvation of the world through Jesus Christ; the gift of the Holy Spirit; anything for which at the particular time it is especially appropriate to give thanks.

Subjects for intercession should include: the universal Church and all its members; all men and the welfare of the world; all nations and all in authority; the concerns of the local community; those who suffer. It may end with thanksgiving for the departed.

The Dismissal should include one or both of the elements of blessing and commissioning for the service of God in the world.

One way of using this outline is as follows:

The Confession from page 5 may be used; the assurance of God's forgiveness may be given by reading a text of scripture or may be embodied in the prayer. The opening prayer or prayers may include the Collect of the Day. The Intercessions may precede the Prayer of Thanksgiving and Dedication, in which case a hymn may be sung between them. The Dismissal is a sending forth of the people to service using such words as those found at the end of the Lord's Supper. It may be combined with or replaced by a blessing.

The Preparation

1 Hymn

2 Prayers of adoration and confession, with an assurance of God's forgiveness

The Ministry of the Word

3   Hymn

4   The Old Testament Lesson, or the Epistle, or both

5   Hymn

6   The Gospel

7   The Sermon

8   The Apostles' Creed (pages 38-9)

9   Hymn

The Response

10   Prayer of Thanksgiving and Dedication (for other forms, see pages 32-7)

> We praise you, God our Father,
> for the world which you created
> and for our place in it.
>
> You have given us life that we may love and serve you;
> and though we have resisted your purpose and misused
> your gift,

you have not left us in our sin,
but have sent your Son Jesus Christ to be our Saviour.

We thank you that for us he became man,
died on the cross,
rose from the dead,
and ascended into heaven;
there he reigns in glory,
and there he prays for us;
and we believe that he will be our judge.

We thank you that you have sent your Holy Spirit
to bring us to a new life in Christ
and give us freedom to call you Father.

(Here special thanksgivings may be offered)

Therefore with all the Church on earth and in heaven,
we give you our thanks and praise.

We dedicate ourselves to you;
strengthen us by your Holy Spirit to do your will,
and bring us with all men to your kingdom,
through Jesus Christ our Lord. **Amen.**

11 Intercessions (for possible forms, see pages 7-9, 24-31)

12 The Lord's Prayer

13 Hymn

14 Dismissal

Appendices

1 The Commandments of the Lord Jesus

Our Lord Jesus Christ said: The first commandment is,
Hear, O Israel:
The Lord our God, the Lord is one; and you shall love the
Lord your God with all your heart, and with all your soul,
and with all your mind, and with all your strength.

**Lord, have mercy upon us, and incline our hearts to keep
this law.**

The second is this, You shall love your neighbour as
yourself. There is no other commandment greater than
these.

**Lord, have mercy upon us, and incline our hearts to keep
this law.**

A new commandment I give to you, that you love one
another; even as I have loved you, that you also love
one another.

**Lord, have mercy upon us, and write all these your laws in
our hearts, we beseech you.**

God spoke all these words saying, Hear the Lord your God;

You shall have no other gods before me.

You shall not make yourself any idol.

You shall not take the name of the Lord your God
in vain.

Remember the sabbath day, to keep it holy.
Six days you shall labour, and do all your work;
but the seventh day is a sabbath to the Lord your God.

**Lord, have mercy upon us, and incline our hearts to
keep these laws.**

Honour your father and your mother.

You shall not kill.

You shall not commit adultery.

You shall not steal.

You shall not bear false witness.

You shall not covet.

**Lord, have mercy upon us, and write all these your laws
in our hearts, we beseech you.**

3 Alternative Intercessions for use whether or not there is Communion (pages 7 and 21)

A

The specific petitions that are indented are suggestions which may be varied as desired.

Let us pray for all men everywhere according to their need.

Let us pray for the Church of Christ throughout the world:
for its unity in Christ
for the fulfilment of its mission
for all ministers of the gospel
for all Christians here in . . .

Silence

Strengthen your Church to carry forward the work of Christ; that we and all who confess your name may be united in your truth, live together in your love, and reveal your glory in the world.

Lord, in your mercy
Hear our prayer.

Let us pray for all the nations and peoples of the world:
for all who serve the common good
for our own country and government, and for all in authority . . .
for those involved in . . .

Silence

Give wisdom to all in authority; direct this nation and all nations in the ways of justice and peace; that men may honour one another, and seek the common good.

Lord, in your mercy
Hear our prayer.

Let us pray for those we know and love:
 for the local community
 for our families and friends
 for . . .

Silence

Give grace to us, to our families and friends, and to all our neighbours in Christ; that we may serve him in one another, and love as he loves us.

Lord, in your mercy
Hear our prayer.

Let us pray for all who suffer:
 for the sick
 for those who mourn
 for those without faith
 for those who serve the needy
 for . . .

Silence

Comfort and heal all those who suffer in body, mind or spirit; give them courage and hope in their troubles; and bring them the joy of your salvation.

Lord, in your mercy
Hear our prayer.

Let us remember all who have died, giving thanks especially for those who have died in the faith of Christ.

Silence

We commend all men to your unfailing love, that in them your will may be done; and we rejoice at the faithful witness of your saints in every age, praying that we may share with them in your eternal kingdom.

Lord, in your mercy
Hear our prayer.

The leader concludes with this or some other prayer:

Almighty God, we pray you to cleanse and defend your Church, and to unite us all in a common bond of love and service; that we may show forth your goodness and reveal your glory; through Jesus Christ our Lord. **Amen.**

B

Let us with one heart and one mind offer our prayers for the whole Church of Christ, and for all men according to their need.

Let us pray

for the peace of the world, that a spirit of respect and understanding may grow among the nations and peoples,
for the governments of the nations, that there may be peace and justice among all men,
for all people in their daily life and work, that they may have joy in doing God's will,
for . . .

Lord, in your mercy
Hear our prayer.

Let us pray

for all who minister to the suffering, the friendless and the needy, that God's purposes may be fulfilled,
for our enemies and all who wrong us, that we may bear a Christian witness,
for the suffering, the sorrowful, the aged and the dying, that they may be strengthened and comforted,
for . . .

Lord, in your mercy
Hear our prayer.

Here any special prayers may be offered.

Let us pray

for the whole Church of Christ, that, professing one Lord, one faith and one baptism, all whom Christ calls may live in the unity of the one Spirit, •
for all who spread the gospel, that they may draw all men to the Father,
for all who receive God's Word, that they may reveal his glory,
for . . .

Lord, in your mercy
Hear our prayer.

The leader concludes with these or some other prayers:

We give you thanks and praise for all your saints. Help us, strengthened by their fellowship, to follow their examples, and bring us with them into the fullness of your eternal joy.

Lord God, holy and faithful, you have called us to your
service; help us to know and to do your will, that we may
be worthy of our calling; through Jesus Christ our Lord.
Amen.

C

The leader makes the following biddings, and in the course of
the pause which follows the people may mention subjects for
prayer:

I ask your prayers for God's family throughout the world,
for all who bear responsibility among his people,
for all ministers of the word and sacraments,
and for all who gather in his name here in . . .

Silence

The Lord hears our prayer.
Thanks be to God.

I ask your prayers for the peace of the world,
for the rulers of all the nations,
for government in accordance with God's holy will,
and for a just and proper use of the natural resources
of the world.

Silence

The Lord hears our prayer.
Thanks be to God.

I ask your prayers for the concerns and activities of this
congregation and of this neighbourhood,
and for ourselves, our families, friends and neighbours.

Silence

The Lord hears our prayer.
Thanks be to God.

I ask your prayers for all in sorrow, need, anxiety or sickness,
for the neglected, the persecuted and the lonely,
and for those in any need or trouble.

Silence

The Lord hears our prayer.
Thanks be to God.

Let us praise God for those in every generation in whom Christ has been honoured, and pray that we also, inspired by their example, may have grace to glorify Christ.

Silence

The Lord hears our prayer.
Thanks be to God.

The leader concludes with this or some other prayer:

Almighty God, to whom our needs are known before we ask, help us to ask only what accords with your will; and those good things which we dare not or in our blindness cannot ask, grant us for the sake of your Son, Jesus Christ our Lord. **Amen.**

D

The leader may make special biddings for prayer:

Let us pray.

Hear us, Father, as we pray for your holy Catholic Church:
make us all one, so that the world may believe.

We pray that every member of the Church may truly and humbly serve you:
grant that your name may be glorified by all people.

Guide and strengthen all ministers of your gospel:
make them faithful in your service.

Inspire and lead all who govern and hold authority in the nations of the world:
establish justice and peace among all men.

Give us courage to do your will in all that we undertake:
reveal the life of Christ within us.

Have compassion on all who suffer from any sickness, grief or trouble:
deliver them from their distress.

We remember those who have died:
Father, into your hands we commend them.

We praise you for all your saints who have entered your eternal glory:
bring us all to share in your heavenly kingdom.

Let us pray in silence for our own needs and for those of others.

Silence

Hear us, Lord:
Lord, hear our prayer.

The leader concludes with this or some other prayer:

Heavenly Father, you have promised to hear what we ask
in the name of your Son:
we pray you to accept and answer our petitions, not as we
ask in our ignorance, nor as we deserve in our sinfulness,
but as you know and love us in your Son, Jesus Christ
our Lord. **Amen.**

4 Alternative Thanksgivings for use when there is no Communion (page 20)

A

The specific thanksgivings that are indented are suggestions which may be varied as desired.

> Let us give thanks to the Lord:
> **for his mercy and love are everlasting.**

> You are worthy to receive our prayers and praises, heavenly Father, eternal Lord God; and with all the Church in heaven and on earth we praise you for your majesty and glory, for your goodness and grace.
> We thank you for the wonders of creation,
> and for the revelation of yourself to men:
> > for your gift of life to us
> > for your mercy and grace throughout our lives
> > for the joy of loving and being loved
> > for all that is true and noble, all that is good and pure.
>
> For these gifts we give you thanks and praise.
> **Lord God, heavenly King, almighty God and Father,**
> **we worship you, we give you thanks,**
> **we praise you for your glory.**

> We thank you that you so loved the world
> that you sent your Son to be our Saviour,
> that whosoever believes in him should have eternal life:
> > for his dwelling among us full of grace and truth
> > for his dying for us on the cross
> > for his rising again to be our eternal priest and king
> > for his promise that he will come again to be our judge.
>
> For the gift of Jesus Christ we give you thanks and praise.

Lord Jesus Christ, Lamb of God,
you take away the sin of the world:
have mercy on us;
you are seated at the right hand of the Father:
receive our prayer.

We thank you for the presence and work of the Holy
Spirit:
    for creating fellowship in the truth
    for sanctifying your family, the Church
    for spreading the gospel throughout the world
    for revealing the things of Christ.
For the gift of your holy and life-giving Spirit we give you
thanks and praise. And so, Father, in his power, we offer
ourselves to be a living sacrifice in your service; strengthen
us to serve you, and gather us and all men to your kingdom;
through Jesus Christ our Lord. **Amen.**

B

Let us give thanks to the Lord our God:
It is right to give him thanks and praise.

Father, you are worthy of praise from every creature,
and we give you our thanks and praise for your goodness
and love.
You formed us in your image,
and set us over the whole world to serve you, our Creator.

But we disobeyed your will, and turned against each other.
Yet you did not leave us.
Again and again you called us to yourself,
and in the fullness of time you sent your only Son
to be our Saviour.
Great and wonderful are all your works, Lord God Almighty;
just and true are all your ways.

He came to dwell among us,
and laid down his life for us.
By his death he has destroyed death,
and by his rising again
he has given us eternal life.
In him you have forgiven our sins,
and made us worthy to stand before you.
In him you have brought us out of darkness
into his marvellous light.
Through him you have made all things new.
Glory to you, our Father, for ever and ever.

And that we might no longer live for ourselves, but for you,
through him you sent the Holy Spirit
as your gift to those who believe,
to complete his work on earth
and to lead us into all truth.

Here any special thanksgivings may be offered.

Father, through Jesus Christ your Son
we have been accepted and made your children
by water and the Spirit.
So through him, we now offer ourselves again to you to be a
living sacrifice to your praise and glory. Amen.

C

Let us with all the company of heaven give thanks to God.

Let us pray.

Father, through Jesus Christ and in the power of your Holy Spirit, receive our thanksgivings:
for the creation of the universe through your Word,
for making man in your own image and likeness,
for the revelation of your purposes through the law and the prophets,
We give you thanks and praise.

For the gift of your Son, Jesus Christ our Lord,
for his lowly birth of Mary and for his baptism in the Jordan,
for his ministry of preaching, teaching and healing,
We give you thanks and praise.

For his steadfast love in going to Jerusalem,
for his agony in the garden of Gethsemane,
for his suffering and death on the cross,
We give you thanks and praise.

For his resurrection from the dead and his ascension to your right hand in glory,
for his eternal intercession for us,
for his promise of his coming again to be our Judge,
We give you thanks and praise.

For the outpouring of your Spirit on the Church,
for the commissioning of your Church to make disciples,
for the spreading of your kingdom throughout the world,
We give you thanks and praise.

Here any special thanksgivings may be offered.

So, Father, we offer ourselves to be a living sacrifice;
through Jesus Christ our Lord,
through whom you give us everything that is good,
who, with you, Father, and the Holy Spirit, is God,
living and reigning for ever. **Amen.**

D

Let us give thanks to God.
Let us pray.

Lord God of all power and might, ruler of all things,
you are worthy to receive glory and praise.
Glory to you for ever and ever.

At your command all things came to be,
the expanse of the universe and this earth for your
creatures to dwell in.
By your will they were created and have their being.

You made man and blessed us with memory, reason and
skill to enjoy and share in all creation.
But we turned against you, and betrayed your trust,
and we turned against one another.
Have mercy, Lord, for we are sinners in your sight.

Again and again you called us to return;
and in the fullness of time you sent your only Son,
born of a woman,
to die for us and to rise again,
to open for us the way of freedom and peace.
By his blood he reconciled us;
by his wounds we are healed.

Through him you have freed us from the slavery of sin,
and have made us a people for your own possession,
exalting him to your right hand on high
and sending upon us your holy and life-giving Spirit.

Here any special thanksgivings may be offered.

So, Father, we offer ourselves to you in thanksgiving.
Strengthen us by your Spirit,
and bring us and all men to your heavenly kingdom.

Accept these prayers and praises
through Jesus Christ our great High Priest,
to whom with you and the Holy Spirit
your Church gives honour, glory and worship,
from generation to generation, world without end. **Amen.**

5 During Communion these or other hymns and texts may be used.

A

Jesus, Lamb of God: have mercy on us.
Jesus, bearer of our sins: have mercy on us.
Jesus, redeemer of the world: give us your peace.

B

Lord, I am not worthy to receive you,
but only say the word and I shall be healed.

EITHER:

I believe in God the Father Almighty,
maker of heaven and earth:

And in Jesus Christ his only Son our Lord,
who was conceived by the Holy Ghost,
born of the Virgin Mary,
suffered under Pontius Pilate,
was crucified, dead, and buried,
he descended into hell;
the third day he rose again from the dead,
he ascended into heaven,
and sitteth on the right hand of God the Father Almighty;
from thence he shall come
to judge the quick and the dead.

I believe in the Holy Ghost;
the holy Catholic Church;
the Communion of Saints;
the Forgiveness of sins;
the Resurrection of the body;
and the Life everlasting.   Amen.

OR:

I believe in God, the Father almighty,
creator of heaven and earth.

I believe in Jesus Christ, his only Son, our Lord.
He was conceived by the power of the Holy Spirit
and born of the Virgin Mary.
He suffered under Pontius Pilate,
was crucified, died, and was buried.

He descended to the dead.
On the third day he rose again.
He ascended into heaven,
and is seated at the right hand of the Father.
He will come again to judge the living and the dead.

I believe in the Holy Spirit,
the holy catholic Church,
the communion of saints,
the forgiveness of sins,
the resurrection of the body,
and the life everlasting.   Amen.

7   The old versions of Glory be to God on high and of the Nicene Creed are to be found on pages B57 and B45 respectively.

The Lord's Supper
or Holy Communion
(1936 Service)

General Directions

1 The text of the first service of Holy Communion in *The Book of Offices* (1936) followed very closely *The Book of Common Prayer* of 1662 and so was directly related to the earliest rites in English. The 1936 service is here retained, with only typographical alterations, apart from the Lord's Prayer, which may be said in any customary form; but the rubrics have been simplified.

2 Hymns and psalms may be inserted at various points.

3 The first Lord's Prayer may be omitted.

4 The Collects, Epistles and Gospels of *The Book of Offices* (1936) could still be used, but for the sake of continuity with other Sundays it would be well to use the Collects, Epistles and Gospels of *Collects, Lessons and Psalms*.

5 The Old Testament Lesson may be read between the Collect of the Day and the Epistle.

6 The Minister has full liberty to pray extempore.

7 The table, with a fair white linen cloth on it, stands in some convenient place.

The Service

1   The Minister may say the Lord's Prayer.

2   The Collect

The Minister says:

> Almighty God, unto whom all hearts be open, all
> desires known, and from whom no secrets are hid;
> Cleanse the thoughts of our hearts by the inspiration
> of thy Holy Spirit, that we may perfectly love thee
> and worthily magnify thy holy Name; through Christ
> our Lord. **Amen.**

3   The Minister reads the Commandments of the Lord Jesus;
and the people after every Commandment ask of God mercy
for their transgression of it for the time past, and grace to
keep it for the time to come, as follows:

> Our Lord Jesus Christ said: The first commandment
> is, Hear, O Israel, the Lord our God, the Lord is one:
> and thou shalt love the Lord thy God with all thy
> heart, and with all thy soul, and with all thy mind,
> and with all thy strength.
>
> **Lord, have mercy upon us, and incline our hearts to
> keep this law.**

The second is this: Thou shalt love thy neighbour as thyself. There is none other commandment greater than these.

Lord, have mercy upon us, and incline our hearts to keep this law.

A new commandment I give unto you, That ye love one another; even as I have loved you, that ye also love one another.

Lord, have mercy upon us, and write these thy laws in our hearts, we beseech thee.

Or the Ten Commandments may be said; and the words in brackets may be omitted:

God spake these words, and said; I am the Lord thy God: Thou shalt have none other gods but me.

Lord, have mercy upon us, and incline our hearts to keep this law.

Thou shalt not make to thyself any graven image, nor the likeness of any thing that is in heaven above, or in the earth beneath, or in the water under the earth. Thou shalt not bow down to them, nor worship them: [for I the Lord thy God am a jealous God, and visit the sins of the fathers upon the children, unto the third and fourth generation of them that hate me, and show mercy unto thousands in them that love me, and keep my commandments.]

Lord, have mercy upon us, and incline our hearts to keep this law.

Thou shalt not take the Name of the Lord thy God in vain: [for the Lord will not hold him guiltless that taketh his Name in vain.]

Lord, have mercy upon us, and incline our hearts to keep this law.

Remember that thou keep holy the Sabbath day. [Six days shalt thou labour, and do all that thou hast to do; but the seventh day is the Sabbath of the Lord thy God. In it thou shalt do no manner of work, thou, and thy son, and thy daughter, thy man-servant, and thy maid-servant, thy cattle, and the stranger that is within thy gates. For in six days the Lord made heaven and earth, the sea, and all that in them is, and rested the seventh day: wherefore the Lord blessed the seventh day, and hallowed it.]

Lord, have mercy upon us, and incline our hearts to keep this law.

Honour thy father and thy mother; [that thy days may be long in the land which the Lord thy God giveth thee.]

Lord, have mercy upon us, and incline our hearts to keep this law.

Thou shalt do no murder.

Lord, have mercy upon us, and incline our hearts to keep this law.

Thou shalt not commit adultery.

Lord, have mercy upon us, and incline our hearts to keep this law.

Thou shalt not steal.

Lord, have mercy upon us, and incline our hearts to keep this law.

Thou shalt not bear false witness against thy neighbour.

Lord, have mercy upon us, and incline our hearts to keep this law.

Thou shalt not covet [thy neighbour's house, thou shalt not covet thy neighbour's wife, nor his servant, nor his maid, nor his ox, nor his ass, nor any thing that is his.]

Lord, have mercy upon us, and write all these thy laws in our hearts, we beseech thee.

4   Here are read the Collect, Epistle and Gospel of the Day.

5   The Sermon may be preached before or after the Nicene Creed.

6   The Nicene Creed, all standing:

I believe in one God, the Father Almighty, Maker of heaven and earth, And of all things visible and invisible:

And in one Lord Jesus Christ, the only-begotten Son of God, Begotten of his Father before all worlds, God of God, Light of Light, Very God of very God, Begotten,

not made, Being of one substance with the Father; By whom all things were made: Who for us men, and for our salvation came down from heaven. And was incarnate by the Holy Ghost of the Virgin Mary, And was made man, And was crucified also for us under Pontius Pilate. He suffered and was buried, And the third day he rose again according to the Scriptures, And ascended into heaven, And sitteth on the right hand of the Father. And he shall come again with glory to judge both the quick and the dead: Whose kingdom shall have no end.

And I believe in the Holy Ghost, The Lord and Giver of life, Who proceedeth from the Father and the Son, Who with the Father and the Son together is worshipped and glorified, Who spake by the Prophets. And I believe one Holy, Catholic and Apostolic Church. I acknowledge one Baptism for the remission of sins, And I look for the Resurrection of the dead, And the Life of the world to come. Amen.

7 The Minister reads one or more of these sentences, and during the reading the Offering is made for the poor. This being brought to the Minister, *he* places it on the Lord's Table.

Let your light so shine before men, that they may see your good works, and glorify your Father which is in heaven.   Matthew 5: 16

Lay not up for yourselves treasure upon the earth, where moth and rust doth corrupt, and where thieves break through and steal: but lay up for yourselves treasures in heaven, where neither moth nor rust doth corrupt, and where thieves do not break through nor steal. Matthew 6: 19, 20

He that soweth sparingly shall reap also sparingly; and he that soweth bountifully shall reap also bountifully. Let each man do according as he hath purposed in his heart; not grudgingly, or of necessity: for God loveth a cheerful giver. 2 Corinthians 9: 6, 7

God is not unrighteous to forget your work and the love that ye shewed toward his Name, in that ye ministered unto the saints, and still do minister. Hebrews 6: 10

As we have opportunity, let us work that which is good toward all men, and especially toward them that are of the household of the faith. Galatians 6: 10

To do good and to communicate forget not: for with such sacrifices God is well pleased. Hebrew 13: 16

Whatsoever ye would that men should do unto you, even so do ye also unto them: for this is the Law and the Prophets. Matthew 7: 12

Inasmuch as ye did it unto one of these my brethren, even these least, ye did it unto me. Matthew 25:40

8 The Minister says:

Let us pray for the whole estate of Christ's Church militant here on earth.

Almighty and ever-living God, who by thy holy Apostle hast taught us to make prayers and supplications, and to give thanks, for all men; We humbly beseech thee most mercifully to accept our alms and oblations, and to receive these our prayers, which we offer unto thy Divine Majesty; beseeching thee to inspire continually the universal Church with the spirit of truth, unity, and concord: And grant that all they that do confess thy holy Name, may agree in the truth of thy holy word, and live in unity and godly love.

We beseech thee also to save and defend all Christian Kings, Princes, and Governors; and especially ELIZABETH our Queen; that under her we may be godly and quietly governed: And grant unto all that are put in authority under her that they may truly and indifferently minister justice, to the restraining of wickedness and vice, and to the maintenance of thy true religion, and virtue.

Give grace, O heavenly Father, to all the Ministers of thy Gospel, that they may, both by their life and doctrine, set forth thy true and lively word, and rightly and duly administer thy holy Sacraments: And to all thy people give thy heavenly grace; and especially to this congregation here present; that, with meek heart and due reverence, they may hear and receive thy holy word; truly serving thee in holiness and righteousness all the days of their life.

And we most humbly beseech thee of thy goodness, O Lord, to comfort and succour all them who in this transitory life are in trouble, sorrow, need, sickness, or any other adversity. And we also bless thy holy Name for all thy servants departed this life in thy faith and fear, beseeching thee to give us grace so to follow their good examples, that with them we may be partakers of thy heavenly kingdom: Grant this, O Father, for Jesus Christ's sake, our only Mediator and Advocate. **Amen.**

9 The Minister says to those who come to receive the Holy Communion:

Dearly Beloved in the Lord, ye that purpose to come to the holy Communion of the Body and Blood of our Saviour Christ, must consider how St. Paul exhorteth all persons diligently to examine themselves, before they eat of that Bread, and drink of that Cup. Judge, therefore, yourselves, brethren, that ye be not judged of the Lord; repent you truly for your sins past; have a lively and steadfast faith in Christ our Saviour; amend your lives, and be in perfect charity with all men; so shall ye be meet partakers of this holy Sacrament. For to the end that ye should always remember the exceeding great love of our Master and only Saviour, Jesus Christ, in dying for us, and the innumerable benefits which by his precious blood-shedding he hath obtained for us; he hath instituted and ordained pledges of his love, for a continual remembrance of his death, to our great and endless comfort. To him therefore, with the Father and the Holy Ghost, let us give continual thanks; submitting ourselves wholly to his will and pleasure, and studying to serve him in true holiness and righteousness all the days of our life.

Ye therefore that do truly and earnestly repent of your sins, and are in love and charity with your neighbours, and intend to lead a new life, following the commandments of God, and walking from henceforth in his holy ways; Draw near with faith, and take this holy Sacrament to your comfort; and make your humble confession to Almighty God, meekly kneeling upon your knees, and saying after me:

Almighty God, Father of our Lord Jesus Christ, Maker of all things, Judge of all men; We acknowledge and bewail our manifold sins and wickedness, Which we, from time to time, most grievously have committed, By thought, word, and deed, Against thy Divine Majesty. We do earnestly repent, and are heartily sorry for these our misdoings; The remembrance of them is grievous unto us. Have mercy upon us, Have mercy upon us, most merciful Father; For thy Son our Lord Jesus Christ's sake, Forgive us all that is past; And grant that we may ever hereafter serve and please thee in newness of life, To the honour and glory of thy Name; through Jesus Christ our Lord. Amen.

10 The Minister says:

Almighty God, our heavenly Father, who of thy great mercy hast promised forgiveness of sins to all them that with hearty repentance and true faith turn unto thee; Have mercy upon us; pardon and deliver us from all our sins; confirm and strengthen us in all goodness, and bring us to everlasting life; through Jesus Christ our Lord. **Amen.**

11 All standing, the Minister says:

Hear what comfortable words our Saviour Christ saith unto all that truly turn to him:

B50

Come unto me, all ye that labour and are heavy laden, and I will give you rest. Matthew 11: 28

God so loved the world, that he gave his only begotten Son, that whosoever believeth on him should not perish, but have eternal life. John 3: 16

Hear also what St Paul saith:

Faithful is the saying, and worthy of all acceptation, that Christ Jesus came into the world to save sinners.
1 Timothy 1: 15

Hear also what St John saith:

If any man sin, we have an Advocate with the Father, Jesus Christ the righteous: and he is the propitiation for our sins. 1 John 2: 1, 2

12 Lift up your hearts.

We lift them up unto the Lord.

Let us give thanks unto our Lord God.

It is meet and right so to do.

It is very meet, right, and our bounden duty, that we should at all times, and in all places, give thanks unto thee, O Lord, Holy Father, Almighty, Everlasting God.

Here follows the proper Preface, according to the time, if there is any appointed. If there is no Preface, the Minister and people immediately say:

Therefore with Angels and Archangels, and with all the company of heaven, we laud and magnify thy glorious Name: evermore praising thee, and saying, Holy, holy, holy, Lord God of hosts, heaven and earth are full of thy glory: Glory be to thee, O Lord most High.   Amen.

On Christmas Day

Because thou didst give Jesus Christ thine only Son to be born as at this time for us; who, by the operation of the Holy Ghost, was made very man, and that without spot of sin, to make us clean from all sin. Therefore with Angels, &c.

On Easter Day

But chiefly are we bound to praise thee for the glorious Resurrection of thy Son Jesus Christ our Lord: For he is the very Paschal Lamb, which was offered for us, and hath taken away the sin of the world; who by his death hath destroyed death, and by his rising to life again hath restored to us everlasting life. Therefore with Angels, &c.

On Ascension Day

Through thy most dearly beloved Son Jesus Christ our Lord; who after his most glorious Resurrection manifestly appeared to all his Apostles, and in their sight ascended into heaven to prepare a place for us; that where he is, thither we might also ascend, and reign with him in glory. Therefore with Angels, &c.

On Whit Sunday

Through Jesus Christ our Lord; who after that he had ascended up far above the heavens, and was set down at the right hand of thy Majesty: Did as at this time pour forth upon the Universal Church thy Holy and Life-giving Spirit: That through his glorious power the joy of the ever-lasting gospel might go forth into all the world: Whereby we have been brought out of darkness and error into the clear light and true knowledge of thee, and of thy Son our Saviour Jesus Christ. Therefore with Angels, &c.

On the Feast of Trinity

Who with thine only-begotten Son and the Holy Ghost art one God, one Lord, in Trinity of Persons and in Unity of Substance: For that which we believe of thy glory, O Father, the same we believe of thy Son and of the Holy Ghost, without any difference or inequality. Therefore with Angels, &c.

On All Saints' Day

Who in the righteousness of thy Saints hast given us an ensample of godly living, and in their blessedness a glorious pledge of the hope of our calling: That, being compassed about with so great a cloud of witnesses, we may run with patience the race that is set before us: And with them receive the crown of glory that fadeth not away. Therefore with Angels, &c.

13 The Minister says in the name of all those who shall receive the Communion, or the People join with the Minister in saying, this prayer following:

We do not presume to come to this thy Table, O merciful Lord, trusting in our own righteousness, but in thy manifold and great mercies. We are not worthy so much as to gather up the crumbs under thy Table.

But thou art the same Lord, whose property is always to have mercy: Grant us therefore, gracious Lord, so to eat the flesh of thy dear Son Jesus Christ, and to drink his blood, that our sinful bodies may be made clean by his body, and our souls washed through his most precious blood, and that we may evermore dwell in him, and he in us. **Amen.**

14 The Minister offers the following prayer:

Almighty God, our heavenly Father, who of thy tender mercy didst give thine only Son Jesus Christ to suffer death upon the Cross for our redemption; who made there (by his one oblation of himself once offered) a full, perfect, and sufficient sacrifice for the sins of the whole world; and did institute, and in his holy Gospel command us to continue, a perpetual memory of that his precious death, until his coming again; Hear us, O merciful Father, we most humbly beseech thee; and grant that we receiving these thy creatures of bread and wine, according to thy Son our Saviour Jesus Christ's holy institution, in remembrance of his death and passion, may be partakers of his most blessed Body and Blood: who, in the same night that he was betrayed, took bread; and when he had given thanks, he brake it, and gave it to his disciples, saying, Take, eat; this is my Body which is given for you: Do this in remembrance of me. Likewise after supper he took the cup; and when he had given thanks, he gave it to them, saying, Drink ye all of this; for this is my Blood of the New Covenant, which is shed for you and for many for the remission of sins: Do this, as oft as ye shall drink it, in remembrance of me. **Amen.**

15 The Minister himself first receives the Communion in both kinds, and afterwards delivers to the other officiating Ministers, if any are present, and then to the people in order, into their hands. And when *he* delivers the bread, *he* says:

> **The Body of our Lord Jesus Christ, which was given for thee, preserve thee unto everlasting life. Take and eat this in remembrance that Christ died for thee, and feed on him in thy heart by faith with thanksgiving.**

And when the Minister delivers the cup, he says:

> **The Blood of our Lord Jesus Christ, which was shed for thee, preserve thee unto everlasting life. Drink this in remembrance that Christ's Blood was shed for thee, and be thankful.**

16 The Minister may dismiss each table of communicants with a suitable Scripture sentence.

17 When all have communicated, the Minister returns to the Lord's Table, and places upon it what remains of the elements, covering them with a fair linen cloth.

18 After silent prayer, the people join with the Minister in the Lord's Prayer, the Minister first saying:

> **And now, as our Lord hath taught us, we are bold to say,**
>
> **Our Father . . .**

19 The Minister offers one of the two prayers following:

O Lord and heavenly Father, we thy humble servants entirely desire thy fatherly goodness mercifully to accept this our sacrifice of praise and thanksgiving; most humbly beseeching thee to grant that by the merits and death of thy Son Jesus Christ, and through faith in him, we and all thy whole Church may obtain remission of our sins, and all other benefits of his passion. And here we offer and present unto thee, O Lord, ourselves, our souls and bodies, to be a reasonable, holy, and living sacrifice unto thee; humbly beseeching thee, that all we who are partakers of this Holy Communion, may be fulfilled with thy grace and heavenly benediction. And although we be unworthy, through our manifold sins, to offer unto thee any sacrifice, yet we beseech thee to accept this our bounden duty and service; not weighing our merits, but pardoning our offences, through Jesus Christ our Lord; by whom, and with whom, in the unity of the Holy Ghost, all honour and glory be unto thee, O Father Almighty, world without end. **Amen.**

Almighty and ever-living God, we most heartily thank thee, for that thou dost vouchsafe to feed us, who have duly received this Holy Sacrament, with the spiritual food of the most precious Body and Blood of thy Son our Saviour Jesus Christ; and dost assure us thereby of thy favour and goodness towards us; and that we are very members incorporate in the mystical body of thy Son, which is the blessed company of all faithful people; and are also heirs through hope of thy ever-lasting kingdom, by the merits of the most precious death and passion of thy dear Son. And we most humbly beseech thee, O heavenly Father, so to assist us with thy grace, that we may continue in that holy fellowship, and do all such good works as thou hast prepared for us to walk in; through Jesus Christ our Lord, to whom, with thee and the Holy Ghost, be all honour and glory, world without end. **Amen.**

20 Then is sung or said by the Minister, the congregation standing and joining with him,

Glory be to God on high, and on earth peace, goodwill toward men. We praise thee, we bless thee, we worship thee, we glorify thee, we give thanks to thee for thy great glory, O Lord God, heavenly King, God the Father Almighty.

O Lord, the only begotten Son, Jesus Christ; O Lord God, Lamb of God, Son of the Father, that takest away the sin of the world, have mercy upon us. Thou that takest away the sin of the world, have mercy upon us. Thou that takest away the sin of the world, receive our prayer. Thou that sittest at the right hand of God the Father, have mercy upon us.

For thou only art holy; thou only art the Lord; thou only, O Christ, with the Holy Ghost, art most high in the glory of God the Father. Amen.

21 The Minister dismisses the people with these Blessings:

Now the God of peace, who brought again from the dead the great Shepherd of the sheep, with the blood of the eternal covenant, even our Lord Jesus, make you perfect in every good thing to do his will, working in us that which is well-pleasing in his sight, through

Jesus Christ, to whom be the glory for ever and ever.
Amen.

The peace of God, which passeth all understanding,
keep your hearts and minds in the knowledge and
love of God, and of his Son Jesus Christ our Lord:
and the blessing of God Almighty, the Father, the
Son and the Holy Ghost, be amongst you and remain
with you always.   **Amen.**

Collects, Lessons and Psalms

These Collects and Lessons are based on the proposals of the Joint Liturgical Group, adapted for Methodist purposes.

1 Three lessons are assigned to the morning in the hope that *The Sunday Service* will be used, but the lessons are recommended for use whether *The Sunday Service* is used or not. In the evening greater flexibility is expected, but two lessons are provided for use where they are desired.

   When the Lord's Supper is usually in the evening, the two tables can be reversed; where it is sometimes in the morning and sometimes in the evening, then on days when it is only in the evening, it is possible either to reverse the two tables or else in the evening to retain the evening lessons (if they include a Gospel) or to use the morning lessons of the other year. Similarly, where there are three services on one day, lessons may be drawn from the other year.

2 When the Holy Communion (1936) is used, the Collects, Epistles and Gospels of *The Book of Offices* (1936) could still be used, but for the sake of continuity with other Sundays it would be well to use the Collects, Epistles and Gospels of this lectionary, even though the Collects are in a different style.

3 When Morning Prayer is used, after the Psalm the Old Testament lesson should be read and then after a Canticle the Epistle or the Gospel or both.

4 The controlling lesson, printed in bold type, should be read wherever possible.

5 The longer versions of the Old Testament passages are for possible use in services where only two lessons are read.

6 The first year began on the Ninth Sunday before Christmas 1970.

7 Except on Christmas Day, Easter Day, Ascension Day, Pentecost and Trinity Sunday, the collects and lessons for the day are replaced by those of confirmation when such a service is held, and if desired they may similarly be replaced by those of baptism or other ordinances of the church or by those for the special days at the end of the table.

8 The Psalms are for optional use at any point in any service where a Psalm is required or desired. Most of the Psalms (and where there are alternatives, at least one) are in the *Methodist Hymn Book* and the number in that book is given in brackets.

Ninth Sunday before Christmas (Fifth before Advent)

The Creation

Almighty God, you have created the heavens and the earth, and made man in your own image: teach us to discern your hand in all your works and to serve you with reverence and thanksgiving; through Jesus Christ our Lord, who with you and the Holy Spirit reigns supreme over all things now and for ever.

First Year	*Second Year*
MORNING	MORNING

Psalm 104: 1–4, 24, 31–35 (MHB 52)

Gen. 1: 1–3, 24–31a	**Gen. 2: 4b–9, 15–25**
(or 1: 1—2: 3)	
Col. 1: 15–20	Rev. 4: 1–11
John 1: 1–14	John 3: 1–8

EVENING	EVENING

Psalm 145 (MHB 61)

Prov. 8: 1, 22–31	Job 38: 1–18
Rev. 21: 15–27	Acts 14: 8–17

Eighth Sunday before Christmas (Fourth before Advent)

The Fall

Almighty God, you have given your Son Jesus Christ to break the power of evil. Free us from all that darkens and ensnares us, and bring us to eternal light and joy; through the power of him who is alive and reigns with you and the Holy Spirit, one God, now and for ever.

MORNING	MORNING
Psalm 130 (MHB 59)	
Gen. 3: 1–15 (or 1–24)	**Gen. 4: 1–10 (or 1–16)**
Rom. 7: 7–12	1 John 3: 9–18
John 3: 13–21	Mark 7: 14–23

EVENING	EVENING
Psalm 86: 1–16 (MHB 44)	
Isaiah 44: 6–17	Jer. 17: 5–14
1 Cor. 10: 1–13	Rom. 5: 12–19

Seventh Sunday before Christmas (Third before Advent)

The Election of God's People: Abraham

Almighty God, your chosen servant Abraham faithfully obeyed your call and rejoiced in your promise that in him all the families of the earth should be blessed. Give us a faith like his, that in us your promises may be fulfilled; through Jesus Christ our Lord.

MORNING	MORNING
Psalm 95; 1–7 (MHB 1; 1–7)	
Gen. 12: 1–9	**Gen. 22: 1–18**
Rom. 4: 13–25	Jas. 2: 14–24
John 8: 51–58	Luke 20: 9–16

EVENING	EVENING
Psalm 1 (MHB 15)	
Isaiah 29: 13–24	Gen. 13: 1–18
Rom. 9: 1–8	Gal. 3: 1–14

Sixth Sunday before Christmas (Second before Advent)

The Promise of Redemption: Moses

Lord God our redeemer, who heard the cry of your people and sent your servant Moses to lead them out of slavery: free us from the tyranny of sin and death, and by the leading of your Spirit bring us to our promised land; through Jesus Christ our Lord.

MORNING	MORNING
Psalm 77 (MHB 42)	
Exod. 3: 1–15 (or 1–22)	**Exod. 6: 2–8 (or 2–13)**
Heb. 3: 1–6	Heb. 11: 17–29
John 6: 27–35	Mark 13: 5–13

EVENING	EVENING
Psalm 48: 1–3, 8–14 (MHB 34)	
Deut. 18: 15–22	Exod. 2: 1–10
Acts 3: 1–26	Heb. 8: 1–12

Fifth Sunday before Christmas (The Sunday before Advent)

The Remnant of Israel

Almighty God, who spoke to the prophets that they might make your will and purpose known: inspire the guardians of your truth, that the many may be blessed through the few and the children of earth be made one with the saints in glory; by the power of Jesus Christ our Lord, who alone redeemed mankind and reigns with you and the Holy Spirit, one God, now and for ever.
Or the Collect of the Twenty-second Sunday after Pentecost.

MORNING	MORNING
Psalm 84 (MHB 43)	
1 Kings 19: 9–18	**Isaiah 10: 20–23**
Rom. 11: 13–24	Rom. 9: 19–29
Matt. 24: 38–44	Mark 13: 14–23

EVENING	EVENING
Psalm 18: 25–32, 35 (MHB 22)	
Gen. 6: 5–22	1 Kings 17: 1–16
Luke 12: 1–7 (or 1–12)	Matt. 6: 24–33

Fourth Sunday before Christmas (Advent 1)

The Advent Hope

Almighty God, give us grace to cast away the works of darkness, and to put on the armour of light, now in the time of this mortal life, in which your Son Jesus Christ came to us in great humility: so that on the last day, when he shall come again in his glorious Majesty to judge the living and the dead, we may rise to the life immortal; through him who is alive and reigns with you and the Holy Spirit, one God, now and for ever.

MORNING

MORNING

Psalm 98 (MHB 8)

Isaiah 52: 1–10
1 Thess. 5: 1–11
Luke 21: 25–33

Isaiah 51: 4–11
Rom. 13: 8–14
Matt. 25: 31–46

EVENING

EVENING

Psalm 93 (MHB 49)

Isaiah 62: 6–12
Luke 12: 35–43

Jer. 31: 7–14
1 Thess. 1: 1–10

Third Sunday before Christmas (Advent 2)

The Word of God in the Old Testament

Eternal God, who caused all holy Scriptures to be written for our learning: help us so to hear them, read, mark, learn, and inwardly digest them, that through patience and the comfort of your Holy Word we may embrace and for ever hold fast the blessed hope of everlasting life, which you have given us in our Saviour, Jesus Christ.

MORNING

Psalm 19 (MHB 23)

Isaiah 55: 1–11 (or 1–13)
Rom. 15: 4–13
John 5: 36–47

MORNING

Isaiah 64: 1–5 (or 1–12)
2 Tim. 3: 14–4: 5
Luke 4: 14–21

EVENING

Psalm 20: 1–7 (MHB 24)

Jer. 36: 1–13
2 Tim. 2: 8–15

EVENING

1 Kings 22: 5–17
Rom. 10: 5–17

Second Sunday before Christmas (Advent 3)

The Forerunner

Almighty God, who sent your servant John the Baptist to prepare your people for the coming of your Son: inspire the ministers and stewards of your truth to turn our disobedient hearts to the law of love; that when he comes again in glory, we may stand with confidence before him as our judge; who is alive and reigns with you and the Holy Spirit, one God, now and for ever.

MORNING

MORNING

Psalm 63: 1–8 (MHB 37)

Isaiah 40: 1–11

Mal. 3: 1–5   (or 3: 1–5 and 4: 1–6)

1 Cor. 4: 1–5

Phil. 4: 4–9

John 1: 19–27

Matt. 11: 2–15

EVENING

EVENING

Psalm 66: 1–2, 16-20 (MHB 39)

Mal. 4: 1–6

Amos 7: 4–15

Matt. 3: 1–12

Luke 3: 1–17

The Sunday before Christmas (Advent 4)

The Annunciation

Heavenly Father, who chose the Virgin Mary to be the mother of our Lord and Saviour: fill us with your grace, that in all things we may accept your holy will and with her rejoice in your salvation; through Jesus Christ our Lord.

MORNING

MORNING

Psalm 116 (MHB 55)

Isaiah 11: 1–9

Zech. 2: 10–13

1 Cor. 1: 26–31

Rev. 21: 1–7

Luke 1: 26–38a

Matt. 1: 18–23

EVENING

EVENING

Psalm 8 (MHB 18)

Isaiah 65: 17–25

Jer. 23: 5–8

Luke 1: 39–56

Rev. 22: 6–17, 20

When this day is Christmas Eve, the evening lessons are:
Psalm 8 (MHB 18)
Zech. 2: 10–13 (or Isaiah 11: 1–9)
Titus 3: 4–7

Christmas Day

The Birth of Christ

MIDNIGHT

Eternal God, who made this most holy night to shine with the brightness of your one true light: bring us who have known the revelation of that light on earth to see the radiance of your heavenly glory; through Jesus Christ our Lord.

Psalm 19 (MHB 23)

Micah 5: 2–4	Micah 5: 2–4
Titus 2: 11–15	Titus 2: 11–15
Luke 2: 1–20	**Luke 2: 1–20**

DAY

All praise to you, Almighty God and heavenly king, who sent your Son into the world to take our nature upon him and to be born of a pure virgin. Grant that as we have been born again in him, so he may continually dwell in us, and reign on earth as he reigns in heaven with you and the Holy Spirit, now and for ever.

Almighty God, who wonderfully created us in your own image and yet more wonderfully restored us through your Son Jesus Christ: grant that as he came to share in our humanity, so we may share the life of his divinity; who is alive and reigns with you and the Holy Spirit, one God, now and for ever.

MORNING   **MORNING**

Psalm 23 (MHB 25) or 85

Isaiah 9: 2–7	Isaiah 9: 2–7
1 John 4: 7–14	1 John 4: 7–14
John 1: 1–14	**John 1: 1–14**

EVENING   **EVENING**

Psalm 18: 25–32, 35 (MHB 22)

Isaiah 60: 13–22	1 Sam. 2: 1–10
Gal. 4: 1–7	Phil. 2: 5–11

The Sunday after Christmas*

The Wise Men

Eternal God, who by the shining of a star led the wise men to the worship of your Son: guide by your light the nations of the earth, that the whole world may behold your glory; through Jesus Christ our Lord.

MORNING

Psalm 72: 1–19 (MHB 40)

Isaiah 60: 1–6 (or 1–22)
Heb. 1: 1–4
Matt. 2: 1–12

MORNING

Isaiah 49: 7–13 (or 1–13)
Eph. 3: 1–6
Matt. 2: 1–12

EVENING

Psalm 67 (MHB 9)

Isaiah 49: 13–23
1 John 1: 1–2: 2

EVENING

Isaiah 61: 1–11
Rom. 15: 13–21

*If this falls on December 30th, the lessons of the Second Sunday after Christmas are read.

Second Sunday after Christmas*

1. *The Presentation in the Temple*
2. *The Visit to Jerusalem*

Almighty Father, whose Son Jesus Christ was presented in the
Temple and acclaimed the light of the nations: grant that in
him we may be presented before you, and through him may
bring light to the world; through Jesus Christ our Lord.

MORNING   MORNING

Psalm 100 (MHB 6)

1 Sam. 1: 20–28 (or 1–28)   Deut. 16: 1–6
Rom. 12: 1–8   Rom. 8: 12–17 (or 12–25)
Luke 2: 21–40   **Luke 2: 41–52**

EVENING   EVENING

Psalm 73: 1–6, 13–26, 28 (MHB 41)

Isaiah 40: 25–31   Hag. 2: 1–9
Col. 1: 1–14   Luke 2: 21–40

  *If this falls on January 6th, the lessons of the Sunday after
  Christmas are read.

Epiphany**

Eternal God, who by the shining of a star led the wise men to
the worship of your Son: guide by your light the nations of the
earth, that the whole world may behold your glory; through
Jesus Christ our Lord.

Psalm 72: 1–19 (MHB 40)

Isaiah 49: 1–13   Isaiah 60: 1–6
Eph. 3: 1–12   Rev. 21: 22—22: 5
Matt. 2: 1–20   Matt. 2: 1–20

**These lessons are read if January 6th falls on a weekday.

First Sunday after Epiphany

The Baptism of Christ

Almighty God, who anointed Jesus at his baptism with the Holy Spirit and declared him to be your Son: send your Holy Spirit upon us who have been baptized in his name, that we may surrender our lives to your service and rejoice to be called the sons of God; through Jesus Christ our Lord.

MORNING	MORNING
Psalm 36: 5–10 (MHB 30)	
1 Sam. 16: 1–13a	Isaiah 42: 1–7 (or 1–12)
Acts 10: 34–48a	Eph. 2: 1–10
Matt. 3: 13–17	**John 1: 29–34**

EVENING	EVENING
Psalm 42: 1–5, 7–11; 43: 3–5 (MHB 32)	
Exod. 14: 5–18	Josh. 3: 1–17
Mark 1: 1–11	Rom. 6: 12–23

Second Sunday after Epiphany

The First Disciples

Almighty God, by whose grace alone we are accepted and called to your service: strengthen us by your Holy Spirit and make us worthy of our calling; through Jesus Christ our Lord.

MORNING	MORNING
Psalm 27 (MHB 27)	
Jer. 1: 4–10 (or 4–19)	1 Sam. 3: 1–10 (or 1–20)
Acts 26: 1, 9–18	Gal. 1: 11–24
Mark 1: 14–20	**John 1: 35–51**

EVENING	EVENING
Psalm 145 (MHB 61)	
Ezek. 2: 1—3: 3	1 Kings 18: 21–39
Matt. 10: 1–15	Acts 9: 1–20

Third Sunday after Epiphany

The First Sign: 1. *The Wedding at Cana*
                 2. *The New Temple*

Almighty God, in Christ you make all things new. Transform the poverty of our nature by the riches of your grace, and in the renewal of our lives make known your heavenly glory; through Jesus Christ our Lord.

MORNING	MORNING
Psalm 84 (MHB 43)	
Exod. 33: 12–23 (or 7–23)	1 Kings 8: 22–30
1 John 1: 1–4	1 Cor. 3: 10–17
John 2: 1–11	**John 2: 13–22**

EVENING	EVENING
Psalm 34 (MHB 29)	
Num. 9: 15–23	Num. 21: 4–9
Mark 1: 21–34	John 3: 1–15

Fourth Sunday after Epiphany

1. *The Friend of Sinners*
2. *Life for the World*

Merciful Lord, grant to your faithful people pardon and peace, that we may be cleansed from all our sins, and serve you with a quiet mind; through Jesus Christ our Lord.

MORNING

Psalm 66: 1–2, 16–20 (MHB 39)

Hosea 14: 1–7
Philem. 1–16
Mark 2: 13–17

MORNING

1 Kings 10: 1–13
Eph. 3: 8–19
John 4: 7–14

EVENING

Psalm 40: 1–11 (MHB 31)

Gen. 32: 3–12
1 Tim. 1: 12–17

EVENING

Zech. 8: 1–8, 20–23
1 John 5: 1–12

Fifth Sunday after Epiphany

1. *The New Dispensation*
2. *Work*

Give us, Lord, we pray, the spirit to think and to do always those things that are right: that we who can do no good thing without you may have power to live according to your holy will; through Jesus Christ our Lord.

MORNING	MORNING
Psalm 89: 1–18 (MHB 45)	
Joel 2: 15–19, 21–22	Lam. 3: 19–26
2 Cor. 3: 4–11	**1 Thess. 5: 12–24**
Mark 2: 18–22	Matt. 20: 1–15

EVENING	EVENING
Psalm 116 (MHB 55)	
1 Kings 21: 1–19	Zech. 10: 6–12
John 3: 22–36	Jas. 5: 7–11

Sixth Sunday after Epiphany

1. *The Right Use of the Sabbath*
2. *The Holy Mountain*

Heavenly Father, whose blessed Son was revealed that he might destroy the works of the devil, and make us the sons of God and heirs of eternal life: grant that we, having this hope, may purify ourselves even as he is pure; that when he shall appear in power and great glory we may be made like him in his eternal and glorious kingdom; where he is alive and reigns with you and the Holy Spirit, one God, now and for ever.

MORNING   MORNING

Psalm 112 (MHB 54)

Isaiah 1: 10–17   Exod. 19: 16–24
1 Cor. 3: 18–23   **Heb. 12: 18–29**
Mark 2: 23—3: 6   John 4: 19–26

EVENING   EVENING

Psalm 111 (MHB 53)

Gen. 18: 20–33   2 Kings 5: 19b-27
Luke 13: 1–9   Matt. 22: 1-14

Ninth Sunday before Easter

Christ the Teacher

Eternal God, whose Son Jesus Christ is for all mankind the way, the truth, and the life: teach us to walk in his way, to rejoice in his truth, and to share his risen life; who lives and reigns with you and the Holy Spirit, one God, now and for ever.

MORNING	MORNING
Psalm 103 (MHB 51)	
Isaiah 30: 18–21 (or 8–21)	Prov. 3: 1–8 (or 1–18)
1 Cor. 4: 8–13	1 Cor. 2: 1–10
Matt. 5: 1–12	**Luke 8: 4–15**

EVENING	EVENING
Psalm 19 (MHB 23)	
2 Sam. 12: 1–14	Job 28: 12–28
Mark 4: 21–34	Matt. 13: 44–58

Eighth Sunday before Easter

Christ the Healer

Almighty and everlasting God, whose Son Jesus Christ healed the sick and restored them to wholeness of life: look with compassion on the anguish of the world, and by your healing power make whole both men and nations; through our Lord and Saviour Jesus Christ, who is alive and reigns with you and the Holy Spirit, one God, now and for ever.

MORNING

Psalm 48: 1–3, 8–14 (MHB 34)

Zeph. 3: 14–20
Jas. 5: 13–16
Mark 2: 1–12

MORNING

2 Kings 5: 1–14 (or 1–27)
2 Cor. 12: 1–10
Mark 1: 35–45

EVENING

Psalm 139: 1–12, 17–18, 23–24 (MHB 60)

2 Kings 4: 18–37
Mark 3: 1–12

EVENING

Job 2: 1–10
Mark 7: 24–37

Seventh Sunday before Easter

Christ, Worker of Miracles

Almighty God, whose Son Jesus Christ fed the hungry with the bread of the Kingdom and the word of his mouth; renew your people with your heavenly grace; and in all our weakness sustain us by your true and living bread; through Jesus Christ our Lord.

MORNING   MORNING

Psalm 46 (MHB 33)

Deut. 8: 1–6 (or 1–10)	Jonah 1: 1–17
Phil. 4: 10–20	Jas. 1: 2–12
John 6: 1–14	**Mark 4: 35–41**

EVENING   EVENING

Psalm 20: 1–7 (MHB 24)

Isaiah 41: 8–16	Isaiah 30: 8–17
John 9: 1–25	Mark 6: 45–56

Ash Wednesday

Almighty and everlasting God, you hate nothing that you have made, and forgive the sins of all those who are penitent. Create and make in us new and contrite hearts, that, lamenting our sins and acknowledging our wretchedness, we may receive from you, the God of all mercy, perfect forgiveness and peace; through Jesus Christ our Lord.

MORNING   MORNING

Psalm 51: 1–4, 9–17 (MHB 35)

Isaiah 58: 1–8 (or 1–12)   Amos 5: 6–15 (or 4–15)
1 Cor. 9: 24–27   Jas. 4: 1–8a
Matt. 6: 16–21   **Luke 18: 9–14**

EVENING   EVENING

Psalm 130 (MHB 59)

Isaiah 1: 10–20   Joel 2: 12–19
Mark 2: 18–22   2 Tim. 2: 1–7

Sixth Sunday before Easter (Lent 1)

The King and the Kingdom: Temptation

Almighty God, whose Son Jesus Christ fasted forty days in the wilderness, and was tempted as we are, yet without sin: give us grace to discipline ourselves in submission to your Spirit; and as you know our weakness, so may we know your power to save; through Jesus Christ our Lord.

MORNING

MORNING

Psalm 51: 1–4, 9–17 (MHB 35)

Deut. 30: 15–20 (or 11–20)
Heb. 2: 14–18
Matt. 4: 1–17

Deut. 6: 10–17
Heb. 4: 12–16
Luke 4: 1–13

EVENING

EVENING

Psalm 91: 1–6, 9–16 (MHB 47)

Jer. 31: 27–34
Mark 14: 1–25

Isaiah 58: 1–8
Luke 22: 1–38

Fifth Sunday before Easter (Lent 2)

The King and the Kingdom: Conflict

Lord God Almighty, whose Son Jesus Christ prayed for his disciples that in all the conflicts of the world you would keep them from the evil one: strengthen us to resist every assault and temptation, and to follow you, the only God; through Jesus Christ our Lord.

MORNING	MORNING
Psalm 18: 1–19 (MHB 21)	
2 Kings 6: 8–17 (or 8–23)	Isaiah 35: 1–10
1 John 4: 1–6	1 John 3: 1–8
Luke 11: 14–26	**Matt. 12: 22–32**

EVENING	EVENING
Psalm 90 (MHB 46)	
Isaiah 59: 1–16	Gen. 37: 12–28
Mark 14: 26–52	Luke 22: 39–53

Fourth Sunday before Easter (Lent 3)

The King and the Kingdom: Suffering

Almighty God, whose most dear Son went not up to joy but first he suffered pain, and entered not into glory before he was crucified: grant that we, walking in the way of the cross, may find it to be the way of life and peace; through Jesus Christ our Lord.

MORNING

MORNING

Psalm 73: 1–6, 13–26, 28 (MHB 41)

Isaiah 59: 15–20 (or 1–21)
1 Peter 2: 19–25
Matt. 16: 13–28

Isaiah 45: 18–25 (or 14–25)
Col. 1: 24–29
Luke 9: 18–27

EVENING

EVENING

Psalm 63: 1–8 (MHB 37)

Jer. 2: 1–13
Mark 14: 53–72

Micah 7: 1–7
Luke 22: 54–71

Third Sunday before Easter (Lent 4)

The King and the Kingdom: Transfiguration

Almighty Father, whose Son was revealed in majesty before he suffered death upon the cross: give us faith to perceive his glory, that we may be strengthened to suffer with him, and be changed into his likeness, from glory to glory; who is alive and reigns with you and the Holy Spirit, one God, now and for ever.

MORNING   MORNING

Psalm 34 (MHB 29)

MORNING	MORNING
Exod. 34: 29–35	1 Kings 19: 1–12 (or 1–18)
2 Cor. 3: 12–18	2 Peter 1: 16–19
Matt. 17: 1–13	**Luke 9: 28–36**

EVENING   EVENING

Psalm 36: 5–10 (MHB 30)

EVENING	EVENING
Isaiah 52: 13—53: 6	Jer. 30: 12–17
Mark 15: 1–20	Luke 23: 1–25

Second Sunday before Easter (Passion Sunday)

The King and the Kingdom: Victory of the Cross

Most merciful God, who by the death and resurrection of your Son Jesus Christ delivered and saved mankind: grant that by faith in him who suffered on the cross we may triumph in the power of his victory; through Jesus Christ our Lord.

MORNING

MORNING

Psalm 130 (MHB 59) or 22

Isaiah 63: 1–9 (or 1–16)	Jer. 31: 31–34
Col. 2: 8–15	Heb. 9: 11–15
John 12: 20–32	**Mark 10: 32–45**

EVENING

EVENING

Psalm 121 (MHB 57)

Isaiah 53: 7–12	Lam. 1: 1–14
Mark 15: 21–41	Luke 23: 26–49

The Sunday before Easter (Palm Sunday)

The Way of the Cross

Almighty and everlasting God, who in your tender love towards mankind sent your Son our Saviour Jesus Christ to take upon him our flesh and to suffer death upon the cross, that all mankind should follow the example of his great humility: grant that we may both follow the example of his passion and also be made partakers of his resurrection; through Jesus Christ our Lord.

MORNING

Psalm 24 (MHB 26)

MORNING

Zech. 9: 9–12
1 Cor. 1: 18–25
Mark 11: 1–11 or
Mark (14 and) 15: 1–39
or **Mark 15: 21–39**

Isaiah 52: 13—53: 12
Heb. 10: 1–10
Matt. 21: 1–11 or
Matt. (26 and) 27: 1–61
or **Matt. 27: 32–54**

EVENING

Psalm 72: 1–19 (MHB 40)

EVENING

Isaiah 56: 1–8
Mark 11: 12–33

Isaiah 5: 1–7
Mark 12: 1–12

Thursday before Easter (Maundy Thursday)

The Upper Room

Almighty God, we thank you that in this wonderful sacrament you have given us the memorial of your Son Jesus Christ. Grant us so to reverence the sacred mysteries of his body and blood that our lives may bear abundantly the fruits of his redemption; who is alive and reigns with you and the Holy Spirit, one God, now and for ever.

Almighty Father, whose Son Jesus Christ has taught us that what we do for the least of our brethren we do also for him: give us the will to be the servants of others as he was the servant of all; who gave up his life and died for us, yet is alive and reigns with you and the Holy Spirit, one God, now and for ever.

Psalm 116 (MHB 55)

Isaiah 52: 13—53: 12	Jer. 31: 31–34
1 Cor. 11: 23–29	1 Cor. 10: 16–17
John 13: 1–15	**Mark 14: 12–26**

Good Friday

The Death of Christ

Almighty Father, look with mercy on this your family, for which our Lord Jesus Christ was content to be betrayed and given up into the hands of wicked men, and to suffer death upon the cross; who is alive and glorified with you and the Holy Spirit, one God, now and for ever.

Almighty and everlasting God, by whose Spirit the whole body of your faithful people is governed and sanctified: hear our prayer which we offer for all members of your holy Church; that each in his vocation and ministry may serve you in holiness and truth to the glory of your Name; through our Lord and Saviour, Jesus Christ.

Almighty God, who called your Church to witness that you were in Christ reconciling men to yourself: help us so to proclaim the good news of your love that all who hear it may be reconciled to you; through him who died for us and rose again and reigns with you and the Holy Spirit, one God, now and for ever.

MORNING	MORNING
Psalm 40: 1–11 (MHB 31)	
Exod. 12: 1–8, 11 (or 1–13)	Exod. 12: 1–8, 11 (or 1–13)
Heb. 10: 11–25	Heb. 10: 11–25
John (18 and) 19: 1–37 or	**John (18 and) 19: 1–37** or
John 19: 17–30	**John 19: 17–30**

EVENING	EVENING
Psalm 42: 1–5, 7–11, 43: 3–5 (MHB 32)	
Job 19: 21—20: 5	Lam. 3: 1–9, 19–33
John 19: 31–42	Luke 23: 50–56

Easter Day

The Resurrection of Christ

Lord of all life and power, through the mighty resurrection of your Son you have overcome the old order of sin and death and have made all things new in him: grant that we, being dead to sin and alive to you in Jesus Christ, may reign with him in glory; to whom with you and the Holy Spirit be praise and honour, glory and might, now and in all eternity.

MORNING

Psalm 118: 14–26, 28–29 (MHB 56)

Isaiah 12: 1–6
Rev. 1: 12–18
Mark 16: 1–8

OR Exod. 14: 15–22
(or 5–30a)
1 Cor. 15: 12–20
John 20: 1–18

EVENING

Psalm 139: 1–12, 17–18, 23–24 (MHB 60)

Isaiah 26: 1–9
Luke 24: 1–12

MORNING

Isaiah 12: 1–6
1 Cor. 5: 7b–8
Matt. 28: 1–10

OR Exod. 14: 15–22
(or 5–30a)
1 Cor. 15: 12–20
John 20: 1–18

EVENING

Isaiah 42: 10–16
Luke 24: 13–35

The Sunday after Easter

1. *The Upper Room Appearances*
2. *The Bread of Life*

Almighty Father, who in your great mercy made glad the disciples with the sight of the risen Lord: give us such knowledge of his presence with us that we may be strengthened and sustained by his risen life, and serve you continually in righteousness and truth; through Jesus Christ our Lord.

MORNING

MORNING

Psalm 145 (MHB 61)

Exod. 15: 1–11 (or 1–18)

Exod. 16: 4–15 (or 1–15, 31–35)

1 Peter 1: 3–9
John 20: 19–29

1 Cor. 15: 53–58
John 6: 35–40

EVENING

EVENING

Psalm 150 (MHB 64)

Num. 13: 1–2, 17–33
2 Cor. 4: 7–18

2 Kings 7: 1–16
Acts 13: 26–39 (or 16–39)

Second Sunday after Easter

1. *The Emmaus Road*
2. *The Good Shepherd*

God of peace, who brought again from the dead our Lord Jesus Christ, that great shepherd of the sheep, by the blood of the eternal covenant: make us perfect in every good work to do your will, and work in us that which is well-pleasing in your sight; through Jesus Christ our Lord.

MORNING

Psalm 111 (MHB 53)

Isaiah 25: 6–9 (or 1–9)
Rev. 19: 6–9
Luke 24: 13–35

EVENING

Psalm 23 (MHB 25)

Jer. 38: 1–13
Rom. 1: 1–17

MORNING

Ezek. 34: 7–15 (or 1–15)
1 Peter 5: 1–11
John 10: 7–18

EVENING

Isaiah 43: 1–7
John 21: 1–14

Third Sunday after Easter

1. *The Lakeside*

2. *The Resurrection and the Life*

Almighty God, whose Son Jesus Christ is the resurrection and
the life of all who put their trust in him: raise us, we pray, from
the death of sin to the life of righteousness; that we may seek the
things which are above, where he reigns with you and the Holy
Spirit, one God, now and for ever.

MORNING

MORNING

Psalm 16 (MHB 20)

Isaiah 61: 1–3 (or 1–11)
1 Cor. 15: 1–11
John 21: 1–14

1 Kings 17: 17–24 (or 8–24)
Col. 3: 1–11
John 11: 17–27

EVENING

EVENING

Psalm 98 (MHB 8)

Neh. 2: 1–18
2 Cor. 1: 1–11

Isaiah 43: 8–21
John 21: 15–25

Fourth Sunday after Easter

1. *The Charge to Peter*
2. *The Way, the Truth and the Life*

Almighty God, who alone can bring order to the unruly wills and passions of sinful men: give us grace to love what you command and to desire what you promise, that in all the changes and chances of this world, our hearts may surely there be fixed where lasting joys are to be found; through Jesus Christ our Lord.

MORNING	MORNING
Psalm 27 (MHB 27)	
Isaiah 62: 1–5 (or 1–12)	Prov. 4: 10–18 (or 1–18)
Rev. 3: 14–22	2 Cor. 4: 11–18
John 21: 15–22	**John 14: 1–11**

EVENING	EVENING
Psalm 77 (MHB 42)	
Isaiah 2: 1–5	Hab. 3: 1–13
1 Peter 1: 10–21	Rev. 1: 4–18

Fifth Sunday after Easter

Going to the Father

Almighty and everlasting God, you are always more ready to
hear than we to pray, and give more than either we desire or
deserve. Pour down upon us the abundance of your mercy,
forgiving us those things of which our conscience is afraid and
giving us those things which we are not worthy to ask save
through the merits and mediation of Jesus Christ your Son
our Lord.

Eternal Father, whose Son Jesus Christ ascended to the
throne of heaven that he might rule over all things as Lord:
keep the Church in the unity of the Spirit and in the bond of
his peace, and bring the whole created order to worship at his
feet, who is alive and reigns with you and the Holy Spirit, one
God, now and for ever.

MORNING	MORNING
Psalm 65 (MHB 38)	
Isaiah 51: 1–6 (or 1–16)	Deut. 34: 1–12
1 Cor. 15: 21–28	Rom. 8: 28–39
John 16: 25–33	**John 16: 12–24**

EVENING	EVENING
Psalm 63: 1–8 (MHB 37)	
Isaiah 51: 12–16	2 Sam. 18: 19–33
Acts 24: 1–21	2 Cor. 5: 1–15

Ascension Day

The Ascension of Christ

Almighty God, as we believe your only-begotten Son, our Lord Jesus Christ, has ascended into the heavens; so may we also in heart and mind thither ascend, and with him continually dwell; who is alive and reigns with you and the Holy Spirit, one God, now and for ever.

MORNING	MORNING
Psalm 8 (MHB 18) or 47	
Dan. 7: 13–14	Dan. 7: 13–14
Acts 1: 1–11	Acts 1: 1–11
Matt. 28: 16–20	**Matt. 28: 16–20**

EVENING	EVENING
Psalm 24 (MHB 26)	
2 Sam. 5: 1–5	Exod. 15: 1–3, 11–18
Heb. 2: 5–18	Heb. 7: 21–28

Sixth Sunday after Easter
(Sunday after Ascension Day)

The Ascension of Christ

Eternal Father, whose Son Jesus Christ, when he returned to glory, did not leave us comfortless, but sent the Holy Spirit to remain with us for ever: grant that the same Spirit may bring us at last to that heavenly home where Christ has gone before to prepare a place, and where with you and the Holy Spirit he is worshipped and glorified, now and for ever.

MORNING	MORNING
Psalm 150 (MHB 64)	
Dan. 7: 9–14	2 Kings 2: 1–15
Eph. 1: 15–23	Eph. 4: 1–8, 11–13
Luke 24: 44–53	**Luke 24: 44–53**

EVENING	EVENING
Psalm 93 (MHB 49)	
Jer. 10: 1–10a	Ezek. 43: 1–7a
Rev. 5: 1–14	Heb. 12: 18–29

Pentecost (Whitsunday)

The Gift of the Spirit

Almighty God, who at this time taught the hearts of your faithful people, by sending to them the light of your Holy Spirit: grant us by the same Spirit to have a right judgement in all things, and evermore to rejoice in his holy comfort; through the merits of Christ Jesus our Saviour, who is alive and reigns with you and the Holy Spirit, one God, now and for ever.

Almighty God, who sent your Holy Spirit to the disciples with the wind from heaven and in tongues of flame, filling them with joy and boldness to preach the Gospel: send us out in the power of the same Spirit to witness to your truth and to draw all men to the fire of your love; through Jesus Christ our Lord.

MORNING	MORNING
Psalm 122 (MHB 58)	
Joel 2: 23–29 (or 21–32)	Joel 2: 28–32 (or 21–32)
Acts 2: 1–11	**Acts 2: 1–11**
John 14: 15–27	John 14: 15–27

EVENING	EVENING
Psalm 104: 1–4, 24, 31–35 (MHB 52)	
Exod. 19: 16–25	Zech. 4: 1–10
Acts 4: 23–37	1 Cor. 3: 16–23

Trinity Sunday (First Sunday after Pentecost)

1. *The Riches of God*
2. *The Church's Message*

Almighty and everlasting God, you have given us, your servants, grace by the confession of a true faith to acknowledge the glory of the eternal Trinity, and in the power of the divine Majesty to worship the Unity: keep us steadfast in this faith, that we may evermore be defended from all adversities; through Jesus Christ our Lord, who is alive and reigns with you and the Holy Spirit, one God, now and for ever.

Almighty and eternal God, you have revealed yourself as Father, Son, and Holy Spirit, and live and reign in the perfect unity of love: keep us steadfast in this faith, that we may know you in all your ways and evermore rejoice in your eternal glory, who are three Persons in one God, now and for ever.

MORNING	MORNING
Psalm 97 (MHB 50)	
Isaiah 6: 1–8	Deut. 6: 4–9
Eph. 1: 3–14	**Acts 2: 22–24, 32–36**
John 14: 8–17	Matt. 11: 25–30

EVENING	EVENING
Psalm 67 (MHB 9)	
Isaiah 40: 12–17	Jer. 18: 1–10
John 5: 17–27	1 Tim. 6: 12–16

Second Sunday after Pentecost (Trinity 1)

1. *The People of God*
2. *The Church's Unity and Fellowship*

Almighty and everlasting God, by whose Spirit the whole body of your faithful people is governed and sanctified: hear our prayer which we offer for all members of your holy Church; that each in his vocation and ministry may serve you in holiness and truth, to the glory of your Name; through our Lord and Saviour Jesus Christ.

MORNING

Psalm 95: 1–7 (MHB 1: 1–7)

Exod. 19: 1–6 (or 1–11)
1 Peter 2: 1–10
John 15: 1–5

MORNING

2 Sam. 7: 4–16 (or 1–17)
Acts 2: 37–47
Luke 14: 15–24

EVENING

Psalm 1 (MHB 15)

Ezek. 37: 15–23
Eph. 2: 11–22

EVENING

Deut. 30: 1–10
Matt. 18: 10–20

Third Sunday after Pentecost (Trinity 2)

1. *The Life of the Baptized*
2. *The Church's Confidence in Christ*

Lord God our Father, through our Saviour Jesus Christ you
have assured mankind of eternal life, and in baptism have made
us one with him. Deliver us from the death of sin and raise us
to new life in your love, by the grace of our Lord Jesus Christ,
in the fellowship of the Holy Spirit.

MORNING	MORNING
Psalm 84 (MHB 43)	
Deut. 6: 17–25	Deut. 8: 11–20
Rom. 6: 1–11	**Acts 4: 5–12**
John 15: 6–11	Luke 8: 41–55

EVENING	EVENING
Psalm 18: 25–32, 35 (MHB 22)	
Prov. 16: 18–32	Prov. 22: 1–12
Matt. 5: 38–48	1 Cor. 1: 1–17

Fourth Sunday after Pentecost (Trinity 3)

1. *The Freedom of the Sons of God*

2. *The Church's Mission to the Individual*

Almighty God, you have broken the tyranny of sin and have sent the Spirit of your Son into our hearts, whereby we call you Father. Give us grace to dedicate our freedom to your service, that all mankind may be brought to the glorious liberty of the sons of God; through Jesus Christ our Lord.

MORNING   MORNING

Psalm 63: 1–8 (MHB 37)

Deut. 7: 6–9a (or 1–11)   Josh. 24: 14–25 (or 1–5, 14–28)

Gal. 3: 26—4: 7   **Acts 8: 26–38**

John 15: 12–15   Luke 15: 1–10

EVENING   EVENING

Psalm 15 (MHB 19)

Jer. 20: 7–13   Ezek. 18: 1–4, 19–23

John 8: 21–36   John 4: 5–26

Fifth Sunday after Pentecost (Trinity 4)

1. *The New Law*

2. *The Church's Mission to all Men*

Almighty God, you show to those who are in error the light of your truth, that they may return to the way of righteousness. May we and all who have been admitted to the fellowship of Christ's religion reject those things which are contrary to our profession and follow all such things as are agreeable to the same; through Jesus Christ our Lord.

MORNING   MORNING

Psalm 19 (MHB 23)

Exod. 20: 1–17   Ruth 1: 8–17, 22 (or 1–22)
Eph. 5: 1–10   **Acts 11: 4–18**
Matt. 19: 16–26   Luke 17: 11–19

EVENING   EVENING

Psalm 48: 1–3, 8–14 (MHB 34)

Deut. 6: 4–15   Jonah 3: 1–10
Matt. 7: 1–12   John 4: 27–42

Sixth Sunday after Pentecost (Trinity 5)

The New Man

O God, since without you we are not able to please you, mercifully grant that your Holy Spirit may in all things direct and rule our hearts; through Jesus Christ our Lord.

MORNING

MORNING

Psalm 112 (MHB 54)

Exod. 24: 3–11 (or 1–18)	Micah 6: 1–8
Col. 3: 12–17	**Eph. 4: 17–32**
Luke 15: 11–32	Mark 10: 46–52

EVENING

EVENING

Psalm 2: 1–8, 10–12 (MHB 16)

Mal. 3: 13–18	Prov. 18: 10–24
Luke 6: 17–26	1 John 2: 7–17

Seventh Sunday after Pentecost (Trinity 6)

The More Excellent Way

Lord, you have taught us that all our doings without love are nothing worth. Send your Holy Spirit and pour into our hearts that most excellent gift of love, the true bond of peace and of all virtues, without which whoever lives is counted dead before you. Grant this for the sake of your only Son, Jesus Christ our Lord.

MORNING

Hosea 11: 1–9
1 Cor. 13: 1–13
Matt. 18: 21–35

MORNING

Psalm 62 (MHB 36)
Deut. 10: 12—11: 1
Rom. 8: 1–11
Mark 12: 28–34

EVENING

1 Sam. 24: 1–17
Luke 6: 27–36

EVENING

Psalm 27 (MHB 27)
Deut. 24: 10–22
1 John 3: 13–24

Eighth Sunday after Pentecost (Trinity 7)

The Fruit of the Spirit

Almighty God, who sent your Holy Spirit to be the life and light of your Church: open our hearts to the riches of his grace, that we may bring forth the fruit of the Spirit in love and joy and peace; through Jesus Christ our Lord.

MORNING   MORNING

Psalm 1 (MHB 15)

Ezek. 36: 24–28 (or 22–32)	Ezek. 37: 1–14
Gal. 5: 16–25	**1 Cor. 12: 4–13**
John 15: 16–27	Luke 6: 27–38

EVENING   EVENING

Psalm 148 (MHB 63)

Isaiah 32: 14–18	Num. 11: 16–17, 24–29
Luke 6: 37–49	Acts 8: 14–25

Ninth Sunday after Pentecost (Trinity 8)

The Whole Armour of God

Almighty God, you see that we have no power of ourselves to help ourselves. Keep us both outwardly in our bodies and inwardly in our souls, that we may be defended from all adversities which may happen to the body, and from all evil thoughts which may assault and hurt the soul; through Jesus Christ our Lord.

MORNING
MORNING

Psalm 18: 1–19 (MHB 21)

Josh. 1: 1–9

1 Sam. 17: 37–50 (or 1–11, 32–50)

Eph. 6: 10–18a
John 17: 11–19

2 Cor. 6: 3–10
Mark 9: 14–29

EVENING
EVENING

Psalm 15 (MHB 19)

2 Sam. 23: 8–17
Acts 19: 23–41

2 Sam. 1: 17–27
1 Thess. 5: 8–24

C50

Tenth Sunday after Pentecost (Trinity 9)

The Mind of Christ

Father of mankind, who gave your only-begotten Son to take upon himself the form of a servant and to be obedient even to death on a cross: give us the same mind that was in Christ Jesus, that, sharing his humility, we may come to be with him in his glory; who is alive and reigns with you and the Holy Spirit, one God, now and for ever.

MORNING	MORNING
Psalm 73: 1–6, 13–26, 28 (MHB 41)	
Job 42: 1–6 (or 38: 1–11 and 42: 1–6)	1 Sam. 24: 9–17 (or 1–17)
Phil. 2: 1–13	**Gal. 6: 1–10**
John 13: 1–15	Luke 7: 36–50

EVENING	EVENING
Psalm 90 (MHB 46)	
2 Sam. 9: 1–13	1 Sam. 18: 1–16
Mark 9: 33–50	Matt. 7: 13–27

Eleventh Sunday after Pentecost (Trinity 10)

The Serving Community

Almighty Father, whose Son Jesus Christ has taught us that what we do for the least of our brethren we do also for him: give us the will to be the servants of others as he was the servant of all; who gave up his life and died for us, yet is alive and reigns with you and the Holy Spirit, one God, now and for ever.

MORNING   MORNING

Psalm 62 (MHB 36)

Isaiah 42: 1–7 (or 1–12)   1 Chron. 29: 1–9 (or 1–16)
2 Cor. 4: 1–10   **Phil. 1: 1–11**
John 13: 33–36   Luke 17: 5–10

EVENING   EVENING

Psalm 91: 1–6, 9–16 (MHB 47)

Exod. 18: 13–26   2 Chron. 24: 8–14
Acts 6: 1–15   Matt. 21: 28–32

Twelfth Sunday after Pentecost (Trinity 11)

The Witnessing Community

Almighty God, who called your Church to witness that you were in Christ reconciling men to yourself: help us so to proclaim the good news of your love that all who hear it may be reconciled to you; through him who died for us and rose again, and reigns with you and the Holy Spirit, one God, now and for ever.

MORNING   MORNING

Psalm 97 (MHB 50)

Isaiah 49: 1–6 (or 1–13)   Micah 4: 1–7
2 Cor. 5: 14–6:2   **Acts 17: 22–31**
John 17: 20–26   Matt. 5: 13–16

EVENING   EVENING

Psalm 30 (MHB 28)

Ezek. 33: 1–9, 30–33   Ruth 2: 1–17
Acts 16: 6–15   3 John

Thirteenth Sunday after Pentecost (Trinity 12)

The Suffering Community

Lord God, whose blessed Son our Saviour gave his back to the smiters and did not hide his face from shame: give us to endure the sufferings of this present time with sure confidence in the glory that shall be revealed; through Jesus Christ our Lord.

MORNING	MORNING
Psalm 48: 1–3, 8–14 (MHB 34)	
Isaiah 50: 4–9 (or 4–11)	Jer. 12: 1–6 (or 11: 18–20 and 12: 1–6)
1 Peter 4: 12–19	**Acts 20: 17–35**
John 16: 1–11	Matt. 10: 16–22

EVENING	EVENING
Psalm 139: 1–12, 17–18, 23–24 (MHB 60)	
2 Kings 19: 8–19	Exod. 5: 1—6: 1
Acts 16: 16–40	Heb. 12: 1–14

Fourteenth Sunday after Pentecost (Trinity 13)

The Neighbour

Almighty God, you have taught us through your Son that love is the fulfilling of the law. Grant that we may love you with our whole heart, and our neighbours as ourselves; through Jesus Christ our Lord.

MORNING	MORNING
Psalm 34 (MHB 29)	
Lev. 19: 9–18 (or 1–4, 9–18)	Deut. 15: 7–11 (or 1–18)
Rom. 12: 9–21	**1 John 4: 15–21**
Luke 10: 25–37	Luke 16: 19–31

EVENING	EVENING
Psalm 62 (MHB 36)	
Prov. 25: 6–22	Deut. 16: 13–20
Luke 14: 7–14	Jas. 3: 13—4: 12

Fifteenth Sunday after Pentecost (Trinity 14)

The Family

Lord God, the protector of all who trust in you, without whom nothing is strong, nothing is holy: increase and multiply upon us your mercy, that, you being our ruler and guide, we may so pass through things temporal that we finally lose not the things eternal. Grant this, heavenly Father, for the sake of Jesus Christ our Lord.

MORNING   MORNING

Psalm 5: 1–5, 7–8, 11–12 (MHB 17)

Isaiah 54: 1–8 (or 1–17)   Gen. 45: 1–15 (or 1–28)
Eph. 5: 21—6: 4   **1 Peter 3: 1–9**
Mark 10: 2–16   Luke 14: 25–33

EVENING   EVENING

Psalm 46 (MHB 33)

Gen. 29: 9–20   Gen. 47: 1–12
Mark 3: 31–35   Luke 10: 38–42

Sixteenth Sunday after Pentecost (Trinity 15)

Those in Authority

Almighty Father, whose will is to restore all things in your beloved Son, the king of all: govern the hearts and minds of those in authority, and bring the families of the nations, divided and torn apart by the ravages of sin, to be subject to his most gentle rule; who is alive and reigns with you and the Holy Spirit, one God, now and for ever.

MORNING	MORNING
Psalm 20: 1–7 (MHB 24)	
Isaiah 45: 1–7 (or 1–13)	1 Kings 3: 5–15
Rom. 13: 1–7	**1 Tim. 2: 1–7**
Matt. 22: 15–22	Luke 11: 1–13

EVENING	EVENING
Psalm 111 (MHB 53)	
Dan. 5: 17–30	1 Kings 12: 1–16
Luke 12: 13–21	Luke 16: 1–13

Seventeenth Sunday after Pentecost (Trinity 16)

The Proof of Faith

Lord of all power and might, the author and giver of all good things: graft in our hearts the love of your name, increase in us true religion, nourish in us all goodness, and of your great mercy keep us in the same; through Jesus Christ our Lord.

MORNING	MORNING
Psalm 23 (MHB 25)	
Jer. 7: 1–7 (or 1–14)	Jer. 32: 6–15 (or 1–15)
Jas. 1: 22–27	**Gal. 2: 20—3: 9**
Matt. 7: 21–29	Luke 7: 1–10

EVENING	EVENING
Psalm 27 (MHB 27)	
Josh. 6: 1–20	Judges 7: 1–8, 19–23
John 6: 53–69	John 7: 1–17

Eighteenth Sunday after Pentecost (Trinity 17)

The Offering of Life

Almighty God, you have made us for yourself, and our souls
are restless till they find their rest in you. Teach us to offer ourselves to your service, that here we may have your peace, and in
the world to come may see you face to face; through Jesus
Christ our Lord.

MORNING

MORNING

Psalm 145 (MHB 61)

Deut. 26: 1–11 (or 1–11, 16–19) Neh. 6: 1–16
2 Cor. 8: 1–9 **1 Peter 4: 7–11**
Matt. 5: 21–26 Matt. 25: 14–29

EVENING

EVENING

Psalm 118: 14-26, 28-29 (MHB 56)

Exod. 32: 1–6, 15–20 1 Chron. 29: 10–20
John 12: 1–8 2 Cor. 9: 1–15

Nineteenth Sunday after Pentecost (Trinity 18)

The Life of Faith

Almighty and ever-living God, increase in us your gift of faith,
that, forsaking what lies behind and reaching out to that which
is before us, we may run the way of your commandments and
win the crown of everlasting joy; through Jesus Christ our Lord.

MORNING	MORNING
Psalm 5: 1–5, 7–8, 11–12 (MHB 17)	
Gen. 28: 10–22	Dan. 6: 10–23 (or 1–23)
Heb. 11: 1–3, 7–16	**Rom. 5: 1–11**
Luke 5: 1–11	Luke 19: 1–10

EVENING	EVENING
Psalm 24 (MHB 26)	
Job 23: 1–10	Deut. 30: 11–20
John 5: 1–16	2 Thess. 2: 13—3: 5

Twentieth Sunday after Pentecost (Trinity 19)

Citizens of Heaven

Merciful God, you have prepared for those who love you such good things as pass man's understanding. Pour into our hearts such love towards you that we, loving you above all things, may obtain your promises, which exceed all that we can desire; through Jesus Christ our Lord.

MORNING	MORNING
	Psalm 122 (MHB 58)
Jer. 29: 1, 4–14	Isaiah 33: 17–22 (or 13–22)
Phil. 3: 7–21	**Rev. 7: 9–17**
John 17: 1–10	Matt. 25: 1–13

EVENING	EVENING
	Psalm 146 (MHB 62)
Ezek. 11: 14–20	Micah 7: 7–10a, 18–20
2 Tim. 4: 6–18	Rev. 21: 10–14; 22: 1–5

Twenty-first Sunday after Pentecost (Trinity 20)

Endurance

Almighty God, your Son has opened for us a new and living way into your presence. Give us pure hearts and steadfast wills to worship you in spirit and in truth; through the same Jesus Christ our Lord.

MORNING

Psalm 121 (MHB 57)

Dan. 3: 13–25 (or 1–25)
Heb. 11: 32—12: 2
Luke 9: 51–62

MORNING

Gen. 32: 24–30 (or 1–30)
1 Cor. 9: 19–27
Matt. 7: 13–20

EVENING

Isaiah 32: 1–8
Heb. 10: 23–39

EVENING

Psalm 67 (MHB 9)

Eccles. 12: 1–14
2 Peter 1: 1–11

Twenty-second Sunday after Pentecost (Trinity 21)

1. *The Holy Mountain*
2. *The Right Use of the Sabbath*

Stir up, O Lord, the wills of your faithful people: that richly bearing the fruit of good works, they may by you be richly rewarded; through Jesus Christ our Lord.

MORNING   MORNING

Psalm 42: 1–5, 7–11; 43: 3–5 (MHB 32)

Exod. 19: 16–24	Isaiah 1: 10–17
Heb. 12: 18–29	1 Cor. 3: 18–23
John 4: 19–26	**Mark 2: 23—3: 6**

EVENING   EVENING

Psalm 62 (MHB 36)

2 Kings 5: 19b-27	Gen. 18: 20–33
Matt. 22: 1-14	Luke 13: 1–9

Twenty-third Sunday after Pentecost (Trinity 22)

1. *Work*

2. *The New Dispensation*

Heavenly Father, whose blessed Son was revealed that he might destroy the works of the devil and make us the sons of God and heirs of eternal life: grant that we, having this hope, may purify ourselves even as he is pure; that when he shall appear in power and great glory we may be made like him in his eternal and glorious kingdom; where he is alive and reigns with you and the Holy Spirit, one God, now and for ever.

MORNING

Psalm 30 (MHB 28)

MORNING	MORNING
Lam. 3: 19–26	Joel 2: 15–19, 21– 22
1 Thess. 5: 12–24	2 Cor. 3: 4–11
Matt. 20: 1–15	**Mark 2: 18–22**

EVENING

Psalm 23 (MHB 25)

EVENING	EVENING
Zech. 10: 6–12	1 Kings 21: 1–19
Jas. 5: 7–11	John 3: 22–36

SPECIAL DAYS

The lessons of All Saints Day are read on 1st November even if it falls on a Sunday. The lessons of the other special days may, if desired, replace the lessons of the day, except on Christmas Day, Easter Day, Ascension Day, Pentecost, and Trinity Sunday.

Watchnight

Psalm 90 (MHB 46)

Eccles. 3: 1–15
Luke 12: 35–50

Deut. 8: 1–20
Luke 12: 13–21

Aldersgate Sunday (May 24th or the preceding Sunday)

Psalm 130 (MHB 59)

Isaiah 51: 1–3, 7–11
Rom. 5: 1–11
Mark 12: 28–37

Isaiah 12: 1–6
2 Peter 1: 1–11
Luke 10: 1–12, 17–20

Education Sunday

Psalm 27 (MHB 27)

Prov. 3: 13–17
Acts 17: 16–34
Luke 2: 41–52

Job 28: 12–28
1 Tim. 4: 9–16
Matt. 13: 44–58

All Saints' Day

Almighty God, you have knit together your elect into one communion and fellowship in the mystical body of your Son. Grant us grace so to follow your blessed saints in all virtuous and godly living that we may come to those unspeakable joys which you have prepared for those who perfectly love you; through Jesus Christ our Lord.

MORNING   MORNING

Psalm 145 (MHB 61)

Isaiah 66: 20–23   Jer. 31: 31–34
Rev. 7: 2–4, (5–8), 9–12   Heb. 12: 18–24
Matt. 5: 1–12   Matt. 5: 1–12

EVENING

Psalm 100 (MHB 6)
Isaiah 25: 1–9
Heb. 11: 32—12: 2

Remembrance Sunday

Psalm 46 (MHB 33)

2 Sam. 23: 13–17   Isaiah 52: 7–12
Rom. 8: 31–35, 37–39   Rev. 22: 1–5
Matt. 5: 1–12   John 15: 9–17
or John 15: 9–17

Christian Citizenship Sunday

Psalm 122 (MHB 58)

Isaiah 58: 1–8   Amos 5: 14–24
Rom. 14: 1–9   Rom. 13: 8–10
Matt. 5: 43–48   Mark 12: 13–17

Overseas Missions

Psalm 67 (MHB 9)

Isaiah 42: 1–9

Rom. 1: 8–17

Matt. 16: 13–19

Isaiah 55: 6–11

Rom. 10: 5–17

John 3: 1–16

Harvest Thanksgiving

Psalm 65 (MHB 38)

Gen. 8: 15–22

Acts 14: 13–17

Mark 4: 1–9

Deut. 26: 1–11

1 Tim. 6: 6–10

Matt. 13: 24–33

Church Anniversary

Psalm 84 (MHB 43)

Gen. 28: 10–22

Heb. 10: 19–25

Matt. 21: 12–16

2 Chron. 7: 11–16

1 Peter 2: 1–5

John 10: 22–29

Canticles

Where Morning or Evening Prayer is not in use, the following Canticles may be sung instead of, or in addition to, the Psalm:

Te Deum (MHB 2), especially on Christmas Day, Easter Day, Pentecost, Trinity Sunday and All Saints Day.

Benedicite (MHB 3), especially from the 9th to the 5th Sundays before Christmas, on the Summer Sundays after Pentecost, and on Harvest Thanksgiving.

Benedictus (MHB 5), in the mornings and *Magnificat* (MHB 7) in the evenings, especially on the Sundays from the 4th before Christmas to the last after Epiphany.

Nunc Dimittis (MHB 10), in the evenings, especially on the Sundays after Christmas and after Epiphany.

The Easter Anthems (MHB 72), especially on Easter Day and the Sunday after Easter.

The Covenant Service

General Directions

1   On 25 December, 1747, and on many other occasions, John
Wesley strongly urged the Methodists to renew their Covenant
with God. His first formal Covenant Service was held in the
French Church at Spitalfields on 11 August, 1755, when he used
the words of Joseph and Richard Alleine which he published in
'The Christian Library'. This service was issued separately in
1780, and was the official Wesleyan form for nearly a century.
Each of the other Methodist traditions developed its own form.
As a result of Methodist union, a single, thoroughly revised,
form was authorized in 1936, and has now been further
revised. In addition to its regular use in Methodism it has been
widely used in other Christian communions.

2   The general custom of the Methodist Church is that this service
is held, save for very special reasons, only once in each year,
usually at its beginning.

3   At whatever time of day this service is held, it is to be regarded
as the principal service and to be used in full.

4   The traditional words, 'Put me to doing, put me to suffering',
do not mean that we ask God to make us suffer, but that we
desire, by God's help, actively to do or patiently to accept
whatever is God's will for us.

The Service

The Preparation

1 Hymn

2 Prayer of Adoration

Let us pray.

Let us adore the Father, the God of love.
He created us;
he continually preserves and sustains us;
he has loved us with an everlasting love, and given us the light of the knowledge of his glory in the face of Jesus Christ.

You are God; we praise you; we acknowledge you to be the Lord.

Let us glory in the grace of our Lord Jesus Christ.
Though he was rich, yet for our sakes he became poor;
he was tempted in all points as we are, yet without sin;
he went about doing good and preaching the gospel of the kingdom;
he became obedient to death, death on the cross;
he was dead and is alive for ever;
he has opened the kingdom of heaven to all who trust in him;
he sits at the right hand of God in the glory of the Father;
he will come again to be our Judge.

You, Christ, are the King of Glory.

Let us rejoice in the fellowship of the Holy Spirit, the Lord, the Giver of life.
By him we are born into the family of God, and made members of the body of Christ;
his witness confirms us;
his wisdom teaches us;
his power enables us;
he will do for us far more than we ask or think.

All praise to you, Holy Spirit.

Silence

3   Confession of sin

Let us humbly confess our sins to God.

God our Father, you have set forth the way of life for us in your beloved Son: we confess with shame our slowness to learn of him, our failure to follow him, our reluctance to bear the cross.

Have mercy on us, Lord, and forgive us.

We confess the poverty of our worship, our neglect of fellowship and of the means of grace, our hesitating witness for Christ, our evasion of responsibilities in your service, our imperfect stewardship of your gifts.

Have mercy on us, Lord, and forgive us.

Let each of us in silence make his own confession to God.

Silence

Have mercy on me, O God, according to your steadfast love; according to your abundant mercy blot out my transgressions. Wash me thoroughly from my iniquity, and cleanse me from my sin. Create in me a clean heart, O God, and put a new and right spirit within me.

4   The Minister stands and says:

This is the message we have heard from him and proclaim to you, that God is light and in him is no darkness at all. If we walk in the light, as he is in the light, we have fellowship with one another, and the blood of Jesus his Son cleanses us from all sin. If we say we have no sin, we deceive ourselves, and the truth is not in us. If we confess our sins, he is faithful and just, and will forgive our sins and cleanse us from all unrighteousness.

Amen. Thanks be to God.

5   The Collect

Father, you have appointed our Lord Jesus Christ as Mediator of a new covenant: give us grace to draw near with fullness of faith and join ourselves in a perpetual covenant with you, through Jesus Christ our Lord. **Amen.**

The Collect of the Day may also be read.

6   Hymn

The Ministry of the Word

7 The Old Testament Lesson

The Book of Jeremiah, the thirty-first chapter, beginning at the thirty-first verse.

Behold, the days are coming, says the Lord, when I will make a new covenant with the house of Israel and the house of Judah, not like the covenant which I made with their fathers when I took them by the hand to bring them out of the land of Egypt, my covenant which they broke, though I was their husband, says the Lord. But this is the covenant which I will make with the house of Israel after those days, says the Lord: I will put my law within them, and I will write it upon their hearts; and I will be their God, and they shall be my people.

8 The Epistle

The Letter to the Hebrews, the twelfth chapter, beginning at the twenty-second verse.

But you have come to Mount Zion and to the city of the living God, the heavenly Jerusalem, and to innumerable angels in festal gathering, and to the assembly of the first-born who are enrolled in heaven, and to a judge who is God of all, and to the spirits of just men made perfect, and to Jesus, the mediator of a new covenant, and to the sprinkled blood that speaks more graciously than the blood of Abel.
See that you do not refuse him who is speaking.

9 Hymn

10 The Gospel

> The Gospel according to John, the fifteenth chapter, beginning at the first verse.

The people may say: **Glory to Christ our Saviour.**

> I am the true vine, and my Father is the vinedresser. Every branch of mine that bears no fruit, he takes away, and every branch that does bear fruit he prunes, that it may bear more fruit. You are already made clean by the word which I have spoken to you. Abide in me, and I in you. As the branch cannot bear fruit by itself, unless it abides in the vine, neither can you, unless you abide in me. I am the vine, you are the branches. He who abides in me, and I in him, he it is that bears much fruit, for apart from me you can do nothing. If a man does not abide in me, he is cast forth as a branch and withers; and the branches are gathered, thrown into the fire and burned. If you abide in me, and my words abide in you, ask whatever you will, and it shall be done for you. By this my Father is glorified, that you bear much fruit, and so prove to be my disciples.

The people may say: **Praise to Christ our Lord.**

11 The Sermon

12 A hymn may be sung.

13 Those who leave do so now, after this blessing:

> The grace of the Lord Jesus Christ be with you all. **Amen.**

The Covenant

14   In the Old Covenant, God chose Israel to be his people
and to obey his laws. Our Lord Jesus Christ, by his death
and resurrection, has made a New Covenant with all who
trust in him. We stand within this Covenant and we bear
his name.

On the one side, God promises in this Covenant to give us
new life in Christ. On the other side, we are pledged to
live no more for ourselves but for him.

Today, therefore, we meet expressly, as generations of
our fathers have met, to renew the Covenant which bound
them, and binds us, to God.

15   This or some other hymn:

Come, let us use the grace divine,
    And all, with one accord,
In a perpetual covenant join
    Ourselves to Christ the Lord:

Give up ourselves, through Jesu's power,
    His name to glorify;
And promise, in this sacred hour,
    For God to live and die.

The covenant we this moment make
    Be ever kept in mind:
We will no more our God forsake,
    Or cast his words behind.

We never will throw off his fear
   Who hears our solemn vow;
And if thou art well pleased to hear,
   Come down, and meet us now.

To each the covenant blood apply,
   Which takes our sins away;
And register our names on high,
   And keep us to that day. Amen.

16   The people stand, and the Minister says:

Beloved in Christ, let us again claim for ourselves this
Covenant which God has made with his people, and take
the yoke of Christ upon us.
To take his yoke upon us means that we are content that
he appoint us our place and work, and that he himself be
our reward.
Christ has many services to be done; some are easy, others
are difficult; some bring honour, others bring reproach;
some are suitable to our natural inclinations and material
interests, others are contrary to both. In some we may
please Christ and please ourselves, in others we cannot
please Christ except by denying ourselves. Yet the power
to do all these things is given us in Christ, who strengthens
us.
Therefore let us make this Covenant of God our own. Let
us give ourselves anew to him, trusting in his promises and
relying on his grace.

17 The people sit or kneel, and the Minister says:

Lord God, Holy Father, since you have called us through
Christ to share in this gracious Covenant, we take upon
ourselves with joy the yoke of obedience, and, for love of
you, engage ourselves to seek and do your perfect will.
We are no longer our own, but yours.

**I am no longer my own, but yours. Put me to what you will,
rank me with whom you will; put me to doing, put me to
suffering; let me be employed for you or laid aside for you,
exalted for you or brought low for you; let me be full, let
me be empty; let me have all things, let me have nothing;
I freely and wholeheartedly yield all things to your pleasure
and disposal. And now, glorious and blessed God, Father,
Son, and Holy Spirit, you are mine and I am yours. So be
it. And the covenant now made on earth, let it be ratified
in heaven. Amen.**

18 The Lord's Prayer

Our Father . . .

The Lord's Supper

19 The Peace

The peace of the Lord be always with you.
And also with you.

20 The Peace may be given throughout the congregation, with
the words:

The peace of the Lord.

D10

21 Hymn

22 Bread and wine are brought to the Minister, or, being already on the table, are uncovered.

23 The Minister takes the bread and wine and prepares them for use.

24 The Minister then proceeds with the Lord's Supper, beginning at the words:

Lift up your hearts.

The Marriage Service

General Directions

1 Persons who desire to be married in the Methodist Church must approach the Minister before giving notice to the Registrar. The Minister shall advise them of the legal preliminaries to the solemnization of marriages, such as the requirements about residence in a given registration district, the parental consent needed by minors, and the three weeks' notice to be given to a Registrar or Registrars before a certificate is issued (twenty-four hours for a certificate with licence). *He* should also inform them, before they approach the Registrar or Registrars, whether the church where the marriage is to take place is registered for the solemnization of marriages without the presence of a Registrar, and ascertain whether there is any impediment to the proposed marriage. Attention is drawn to the current regulations of Conference which govern the remarriage of divorced persons.

2 For the purpose of law, the Minister may not proceed with the ceremony until *he* is in possession of a valid certificate or certificates (with or without licence) relating to the marriage.

3 In addition to making preparations for the carrying out of the service and indicating to the couple what they will have to say and do during the ceremony, the Minister shall ensure that the Christian understanding of marriage and its obligations is explained to the couple. The text of the Marriage Service is designed to be used for this purpose.

4 This version of the Marriage Service is so constructed that it may take one of three forms:
   (a) With the Lessons and Address (items 8 and 9) before the Vows;

(b) With the Lessons before the Vows, and the Address between the Pronouncement of the Marriage and the Intercessions;

(c) With the Lessons and Address between the Pronouncement of the Marriage and the Intercessions, after item 21 of the text.

5 If desired the Christian names only of the parties may be used, except in the Declaration of Purpose and in the legally required forms set out in **bold** type, where the full names must be used.

6 The Minister shall see to it that the marriage is recorded in the Register supplied by the Registrar-General, and in the manner stipulated in his instructions.

7 It is permitted, when the parties request it, for two ceremonies to take place in churches of different denominations, and both ceremonies are valid so long as they take place on the same day and the necessary preliminaries as regards each ceremony are complied with.

8 Other legal provisions may apply outside England.

The Marriage Service and The Blessing of a Marriage previously solemnized

Persons who have previously contracted marriage by a civil ceremony in a register office may request a Minister to read the *Marriage Service* (preferably without repeating the vows which have already been made), or to perform the *Service for the Blessing of a Marriage previously solemnized*. Subject to the Standing Orders of Conference the Minister may take either course, after *he* has seen the Certificate of Marriage.

Inter-Faith Marriages

1   The Minister should discuss fully with the parties the religious, domestic and social implications of a marriage between a Christian and a member of another religion.

2   The normal practice should be to supplement a ceremony in the Register Office by prayers in the home. Such prayers should not take the form of the Service of Blessing. This practice accords with that of most overseas Churches in countries from which members of other faiths have come. (Any suggestions that the Service of Blessing creates less difficulty for such a 'mixed marriage' than the Marriage Service is ruled out on the grounds that the Christian content of the two services is identical.)

3   None the less it is recognized that the result of the pastoral counselling involved in (1) may be that both parties desire the Marriage Service. In this event, the following conditions are suggested:
(a) The non-Christian partner respects the Christian convictions of the other partner and his/her right both to practise the Christian faith and to seek to bring up any children of the marriage in this faith.
(b) The non-Christian partner, having read the Service, has expressed willingness to take part in it.
(c) Nothing should be *added* to the structure of the Service.
(d) The *omissions* in the Service should be minimal, and have regard only to what the non-Christian partner cannot say in good conscience.
This might involve the following omissions:
In the Marriage Service, item 19 the final words: 'in the Name of the Father, and of the Son, and of the Holy Spirit'.
In the Blessing of a Marriage, item 13 the first phrase: 'In the Name of the Father, and of the Son, and of the Holy Spirit', and the word 'Christian'.

E3

The Service

1   The persons to be married stand together, the woman on the left hand of the man, in the presence of at least two witnesses.

2   A hymn or psalm may be sung.

The Declaration of Purpose

3   The people standing, the Minister says:

We are gathered here in the presence of God to witness the marriage of *A.B.* and *C.D.*, to support them with our prayers, and to share their joy.

Marriage is given by God. It is not to be entered upon or thought of lightly or selfishly; but responsibly and in the love of God.

According to the teaching of Christ, marriage is the life-long union in body, mind and spirit, of one man and one woman. It is his will that in marriage the love of man and woman should be fulfilled in the wholeness of their life together, in mutual companionship, helpfulness and care. By the help of God this love grows and deepens with the years. Such marriage is the foundation of true family life, and, when blessed with the gift of children, is God's chosen way for the continuance of mankind and the bringing up of children in security and trust. The union of husband and wife is in Scripture compared to the union of Christ and his Church, for he loved the Church and gave himself for it.

A.B. and *C.D.* are now to marry each other, and to seek God's blessing for their married life. If anyone knows of any reason why they may not lawfully marry, let him now declare it.

E4

The Legal Declarations

4 The Minister says to the persons who are to be married:

> I require and charge you both in the presence of God and of this congregation that if either of you knows anything to prevent you from being lawfully married you do now confess it.

5 The man says in the presence of the authorized person (or the Registrar) and two witnesses, as required by law:

> **I do solemnly declare that I know not of any lawful impediment why I, A.B., may not be joined in matrimony to C.D.**

The woman says, in the presence of the same persons, as required by law:

> **I do solemnly declare that I know not of any lawful impediment why I, C.D., may not be joined in matrimony to A.B.**

The Collect

6 The Minister says:

> Let us pray.
> Almighty God,
> to whom all hearts are open,
> all desires known,
> and from whom no secrets are hid:
> cleanse the thoughts of our hearts
> by the inspiration of your Holy Spirit,
> that we may perfectly love you,
> and worthily magnify your holy Name,
> through Christ our Lord.   **Amen.**

The Confession

7   The Minister (or the Minister and the people together) may say:

> O God, your generous love surrounds us,
> and everything we enjoy comes from you.
> We confess our ingratitude for your goodness
> and our selfishness in using your gifts.
> We ask you to forgive us,
> and to fill us with true thankfulness,
> through Jesus Christ our Saviour,
> whom with you and the Holy Spirit
> we praise and worship for ever.   **Amen.**

The Ministry of the Word

(If desired, the whole of this Section, or the Address only, may be deferred and used after item 21, as explained in the General Directions.)

8   The Minister reads:

Matthew 19:4-6

> Jesus said: 'Have you not read that he who made them from the beginning made them male and female, and said, "For this reason a man shall leave his father and mother and be joined to his wife, and the two shall become one"? So they are no longer two but one. What therefore God has joined together, let no man put asunder.'

and one or more of such passages as these:

1 Corinthians 13:4-13

Love is patient and kind; love is not jealous or boastful; it is not arrogant or rude. Love does not insist on its own way; it is not irritable or resentful; it does not rejoice at wrong but rejoices in the right. Love bears all things, believes all things, hopes all things, endures all things. Love never ends; as for prophecies, they will pass away; as for tongues, they will cease; as for knowledge, it will pass away. For our knowledge is imperfect and our prophecy is imperfect; but when the perfect comes, the imperfect will pass away. When I was a child, I spoke like a child, I thought like a child, I reasoned like a child; when I became a man, I gave up childish ways. For now we see in the mirror dimly, but then face to face. Now I know in part; then I shall understand fully, even as I have been fully understood. So faith, hope, love abide, these three, but the greatest of these is love.

Ephesians 3:14-19

For this reason I bow my knees before the Father, from whom every family in heaven and earth is named, that according to the riches of his glory he may grant you to be strengthened with might through his Spirit in the inner man, and that Christ may dwell in your hearts through faith; that you, being rooted and grounded in love, may have power to comprehend with all the saints what is the breadth and length and height and depth, and to know the love of Christ which surpasses knowledge, that you may be filled with all the fullness of God.

Colossians 3:12-16a, 17

Put on then, as God's chosen ones, holy and beloved, compassion, kindness, lowliness, meekness, and patience, forbearing one another and, if one has a complaint against another, forgiving each other; as the Lord has forgiven you, so you also must forgive. And above all these put on love, which binds everything together in perfect harmony. And let the peace of Christ rule in your hearts, to which indeed you were called in the one body. And be thankful. Let the word of Christ dwell in you richly. And whatever you do, in word or deed, do everything in the name of the Lord Jesus, giving thanks to God the Father through him.

9   The Address may follow here.

The Vows

10   All stand and the Minister says:

O God, as you have brought *A.* and *C.* together in love and trust, enable them through the power of your Holy Spirit to make and keep their vows, through Jesus Christ our Lord. **Amen.**

11   The Minister says to the man:

A.B., will you take this woman to be your lawful wedded wife, to live together according to the law of God in the holy estate of marriage? Will you love her, honour and keep her, and forsaking all others be faithful to her so long as you both shall live?

12   The man answers:

I will.

13 The Minister says to the woman:

> *C.D.*, will you take this man to be your lawful wedded husband, to live together according to the law of God in the holy estate of marriage? Will you love him, honour and keep him, and forsaking all others be faithful to him so long as you both shall live?

14 The woman answers:

> I will.

15 *The Minister may say:

> **Who gives this woman to be married to this man?**

Then the father or friend answers:

> I do.

16 The Minister joins the right hand of the woman to the right hand of the man, who says in the presence of the authorized person (or the Registrar) and the two witnesses:

> **I call upon these persons here present to witness that I, A.B., do take thee, C.D., to be my lawful wedded wife,†** to have and to hold from this day forward, for better for worse, for richer for poorer, in sickness and in health, to love and to cherish, till death us do part, according to God's holy law; and to this I pledge myself.

17 They loose hands, and the woman takes the right hand of the man in her right hand and says in the presence of the same persons:

> **I call upon these persons here present to witness that I, C.D., do take thee, A.B., to be my lawful wedded husband,†** to have and to hold from this day forward, for better for

---

* *The following question and answer are optional.*
† *The words printed in bold are required by law.*

worse, for richer for poorer, in sickness and in health, to love and to cherish, till death us do part, according to God's holy law; and to this I pledge myself.

The Giving of the Ring(s)

18   The man and the woman loose hands, and the ring(s) are laid on the book; and the Minister taking it (them) says:

Bless, Lord, the giving of this ring (*these rings*), that he who gives it and she who wears it (*they who wear them*) may ever be faithful one to the other, and continue together in love, as long as they both shall live, through Jesus Christ our Lord. **Amen.**

19   The Minister gives the ring to the man, who puts it on the fourth finger of the woman's left hand. (The woman may in the same way give a ring to the man.) The man and the woman say together:

With this ring (*these rings*) we pledge ourselves to each other, in the Name of the Father, and of the Son, and of the Holy Spirit.

The Pronouncement of the Marriage

20   The Minister joins their right hands and says:

A.B. and *C.D.* have together made their covenant before God and this company; they have made their vows to each other, and have shown their consent by joining their hands and by giving and receiving a ring (*rings*). I therefore pronounce them to be husband and wife, in the Name of the Father, and of the Son, and of the Holy Spirit. Those whom God has joined together let no man put asunder.

God the Father, God the Son, God the Holy Spirit, bless, protect and guide you.
The Lord pour out the riches of his grace upon you, that you may live together in his peace, and finally, by his mercy, obtain everlasting life. **Amen.**

21   A hymn or psalm may be sung.

The whole of The Ministry of the Word, or the Address only, may come at this point.

The Intercessions

22   The Minister says:

> **Let us pray.**

He may here use one or more of the Additional Prayers. Then *he* leads this prayer of Intercession:

> **All grace comes from you, O God,**
> **and you alone are the source of eternal life.**
> **Bless your servants *A.* and *C.***
> **That they may faithfully live together**
> **to the end of their lives.**

Be with them in all their happiness
That your joy may be in them, and their joy may be full.

Strengthen them in every time of trouble.
**That they may carry each other's burdens
and so fulfil the law of Christ.**

Let your blessing be on their home
That your peace may dwell there.

Let it be a place of welcome
That its happiness may be freely shared.

Bless the families and friends of *A*. and *C*.
That we may be united in love and friendship.

Now to him who is able to keep you from falling
and to present you faultless before the presence of
his glory with rejoicing,
**To the only God, our Saviour, through Jesus Christ
our Lord, be glory, majesty, dominion and authority,
both now and for ever.   Amen.**

23   The Lord's Prayer

     Our Father . . .

24   The Lord's Supper may follow here. Otherwise this Thanksgiving follows or the Minister may give thanks in *his* own words.

The Thanksgiving

25   All stand and the Minister says:

Praise God, King of the Universe, who has created all things, and man in his own image.

Praise God, who has created courtship and marriage, joy and gladness, feasting and laughter, pleasure and delight, love, brotherhood, peace and fellowship.

Praise God, who has sent Jesus Christ to save us from sin and redeem our love from selfishness, and has given us the Holy Spirit to make us one with each other and with him.

And so with all the company of heaven we join in the unending hymn of praise:

Holy, holy, holy Lord,
God of power and might,
heaven and earth are full of your glory.
Hosanna in the highest.

The Blessing

26   The Minister says this or some other blessing:

The grace of the Lord Jesus Christ, and the love of God, and the fellowship of the Holy Spirit, be with you all.
                                                              Amen.

Service for the Blessing of a Marriage previously solemnized

General Directions

1　This form of service must not be used for the solemnization of a marriage.

2　Notice of an intended Service of Blessing is not to be given to any Registrar; but the husband and wife should give notice of their wish to the Minister in sufficient time for him to explain to them the Christian understanding of marriage and its obligations.

3　A Service of Blessing must not be recorded in marriage register books supplied by the Registrar-General.

The Service

1　The persons whose marriage is to be blessed stand before the Minister, the wife on the left hand of her husband.

2　A hymn or psalm may be sung.

E14

The Declaration of Purpose

3 The people standing, the Minister says:

We are gathered here in the presence of God because *A.* and *C.*, who are already married to each other, wish to ask God's blessing upon their marriage.

According to the teaching of Christ, marriage is the lifelong union in body, mind and spirit, of one man and one woman. It is his will that in marriage the love of man and woman should be fulfilled in the wholeness of their life together, in mutual companionship, helpfulness and care. By the help of God this love grows and deepens with the years. Such marriage is the foundation of true family life and, when blessed with the gift of children, it is God's chosen way for the continuance of mankind and the bringing up of children in security and trust. The union of husband and wife is in Scripture compared to the union of Christ and his Church, for he loved the Church and gave himself for it.

The Collect

4 The Minister says:

Almighty God,
to whom all hearts are open,
all desires known,
and from whom no secrets are hid:
cleanse the thoughts of our hearts
by the inspiration of your Holy Spirit,
that we may perfectly love you,
and worthily magnify your holy Name,
through Christ our Lord.   **Amen.**

The Confession

5 The Minister (or the Minister and the people together) may say:

> O God, your generous love surrounds us,
> and everything that we enjoy comes from you.
> We confess our ingratitude for your goodness,
> and our selfishness in using your gifts.
> We ask you to forgive us,
> and to fill us with true thankfulness,
> through Jesus Christ our Saviour,
> whom with you and the Holy Spirit
> we praise and worship for ever.   **Amen.**

The Ministry of the Word

6 The Minister reads:

Matthew 19:4-6

> Jesus said: 'Have you not read that he who made them
> from the beginning made them male and female, and said,
> "For this reason a man shall leave his father and mother
> and be joined to his wife, and the two shall become one"?
> So they are no longer two but one. What therefore God
> has joined together, let no man put asunder.'

and one or more of such passages as these.

1 Corinthians 13:4-13

Love is patient and kind; love is not jealous or boastful; it is not arrogant or rude. Love does not insist on its own way; it is not irritable or resentful; it does not rejoice at wrong but rejoices in the right. Love bears all things, believes all things, hopes all things, endures all things. Love never ends; as for prophecies, they will pass away; as for tongues, they will cease; as for knowledge, it will pass away. For our knowledge is imperfect and our prophecy is imperfect; but when the perfect comes, the imperfect will pass away. When I was a child, I spoke like a child, I thought like a child, I reasoned like a child; when I became a man, I gave up childish ways. For now we see in the mirror dimly, but then face to face. Now I know in part; then I shall understand fully, even as I have been fully understood. So faith, hope, love abide, these three, but the greatest of these is love.

Ephesians 3:14-19

For this reason I bow my knees before the Father, from whom every family in heaven and earth is named, that according to the riches of his glory he may grant you to be strengthened with might through his Spirit in the inner man, and that Christ may dwell in your hearts through faith; that you, being rooted and grounded in love, may have power to comprehend with all the saints what is the breadth and length and height and depth, and to know the love of Christ which surpasses knowledge, that you may be filled with all the fullness of God.

Colossians 3:12-16a, 17

Put on then, as God's chosen ones, holy and beloved, compassion, kindness, lowliness, meekness, and patience, forbearing one another and, if one has a complaint against another, forgiving each other; as the Lord has forgiven you, so you also must forgive. And above all these put on love, which binds everything together in perfect harmony. And let the peace of Christ rule in your hearts, to which indeed you were called in the one body. And be thankful. Let the word of Christ dwell in you richly. And whatever you do, in word or deed, do everything in the name of the Lord Jesus, giving thanks to God the Father through him.

7 The Address may follow here.

The Vows

8 All stand and the Minister says to the husband:

A., you have taken this woman to be your lawful wedded wife. Since you wish to acknowledge before God your desire that your married life should be according to his will, I ask you, therefore, will you love her, honour and keep her, and be faithful to her, so long as you both shall live?

9 The husband answers:

With God's help I will.

10   The Minister says to the wife:

C., you have taken this man to be your lawful wedded husband. Since you wish to acknowledge before God your desire that your married life should be according to his will, I ask you, therefore, will you love him, honour and keep him, and be faithful to him, so long as you both shall live?

11   The wife answers:

With God's help I will.

The Prayer over the Ring(s)

12   The husband and wife join their hands; the Minister places *his* hand upon the ring(s) and says:

Let us pray.

Grant, Lord, that he who has given this ring, and she who wears it (*they who have exchanged rings*) may be ever faithful one to the other, and continue together in love, as long as they both shall live, through Jesus Christ our Lord. **Amen.**

13   The husband and wife join their right hands and say together:

In the Name of the Father, and of the Son, and of the Holy Spirit, we acknowledge that God has bound us together, in Christian marriage, for better for worse, for richer for poorer, in sickness and in health, till death us do part.

14   The Minister, holding their joined hands together, says:

Those whom God has joined together, let no man put asunder.

The Blessing of the Marriage

15   The husband and wife kneel, and the Minister says:

> God the Father, God the Son, God the Holy Spirit, bless, protect and guide you.
> The Lord pour out the riches of his grace upon you, that you may live together in his peace, and finally, by his mercy, obtain everlasting life. **Amen.**

The Intercessions

16   The Minister says:

> Let us pray.

He may here use one or more of the Additional Prayers. Then *he* leads this prayer of Intercession:

> All grace comes from you, O God,
> and you alone are the source of eternal life.
> Bless your servants *A.* and *C.*
> **That they may faithfully live together**
> **to the end of their lives.**
>
> Be with them in all their happiness
> **That your joy may be in them, and their joy may be full.**
>
> Strengthen them in every time of trouble
> **That they may carry each other's burdens,**
> **and so fulfil the law of Christ.**
>
> Let your blessing be upon their home
> **That your peace may dwell there.**

Let it be a place of welcome
That its happiness may be freely shared.

Bless the families and friends of *A.* and *C.*
That we may be united in love and friendship.

Now to him who is able to keep you from falling
and to present you faultless before the presence
of his glory with rejoicing,
**To the only God, our Saviour, through Jesus Christ
our Lord, be glory, majesty, dominion and authority,
both now and for ever.   Amen.**

17   The Minister may further pray in *his* own words.

18   The Lord's Prayer.
Our Father . . .

19   The Lord's Supper may follow here. Otherwise this Thanksgiving follows or the Minister may give thanks in *his* own words.

The Thanksgiving

20   All stand and the Minister says:
Praise God, King of the Universe, who has created all things, and man in his own image.
Praise God, who has created courtship and marriage, joy and gladness, feasting and laughter, pleasure and delight, love, brotherhood, peace and fellowship.
Praise God, who has sent Jesus Christ to save us from sin and redeem our love from selfishness, and has given us the Holy Spirit, to make us one with each other and with him.

And so with all the company of heaven we join in the unending hymn of praise:

Holy, holy, holy Lord,
God of power and might,
heaven and earth are full of your glory.
Hosanna in the highest.

The Blessing

21   The Minister says:

The grace of the Lord Jesus Christ, and the love of God, and the fellowship of the Holy Spirit, be with you all.

Amen.

Additional Prayers

These prayers may be used at the indicated places in the Marriage Service or in the Service of a Blessing of a Marriage, at the discretion of the Minister in consultation with the parties to the marriage.

For Christian Family Life

Blessed Lord, the author and giver of all good things, in whom is fullness of joy, send down your blessing, we beseech you, upon your servants whom you have joined as man and wife. Surround them with your good gifts. Bless them in each other, and both in the knowledge of Christ your Son our Lord. **Amen.**

O God our Father, we thank you for uniting *A*. and *C*. in love. Watch over them, guide and protect them, and give them faith and patience; that all their days they may draw strength from you and from each other, through Jesus Christ our Lord. **Amen.**

O Lord our God, help *A*. and *C*. to maintain love and faithfulness to each other as long as they live. May their vows be strengthened and confirmed by your power, so that all their hopes may be fulfilled in accordance with your will. **Amen.**

For the Gift of Children

O Father, in whom all parenthood has its beginning, in whom we live, and through whose power we share the work of creation, we pray for this husband and wife, that they may receive the gift of children, and with the help of your Holy Spirit may bring up their family in the Christian faith and life. We ask this through Jesus Christ our Lord.

Amen.

We pray for *A.* and *C.*, that in their marriage all your will for them may be fulfilled; bestow upon them the gift and heritage of children; and endue them with all the gifts and graces needed for wise parenthood; through Jesus Christ our Lord. **Amen.**

For Concerns outside the Family

O Lord Jesus Christ, who on the cross remembered your mother and your friend, make our homes to be homes of love. Spread your grace over every relationship of human life, so that all our earthly love may be gathered up into the love of God. **Amen.**

O Lord Jesus Christ, from whom we learn that true love is unselfish, help us at this time of our rejoicing to remember the lonely, the bereaved, and those whose homes are broken. **Amen.**

When there are Children already in the Family

O God our Father, we thank you for our children; and we ask that we may so show our love and thankfulness that the example of our lives and teaching may guide them in the way of righteousness and love, through Jesus Christ our Lord. **Amen.**

Almighty God our Father, whose Son Jesus Christ shared the life of the home at Nazareth, grant that marriage may be held in honour among us. Grant that parents and children may live together in peace and understanding; and make every Christian home a school of truth and goodness, through Jesus Christ, who entered an earthly family to bring us heavenly life. **Amen.**

For additional prayers the Minister may draw on other sources or use *his* own words.

The Burial or Cremation of the Dead

General Directions

1 The service has a basic structure, but also a number of variations introduced by the words 'The Minister may . . .' Therefore it is flexible enough for use in a variety of circumstances, yet easily recognized as the same service on all occasions.

2 The first group of prayers provides adequate choice for normal occasions; but there are sometimes circumstances in which the first three Additional Prayers may be more suitable.

3 When the service in church takes place in the presence of a congregation which will not be present at the committal, it is appropriate that one or more of the Additional Prayers should be said after the Thanksgiving, or the minister may pray in *his* own words.

4 It is fitting that in the introduction to the Ministry of the Word the full name and surname of the deceased should be used, but in the Commendation only his baptismal name or names.

5 The first form of the Committal is provided for use on most occasions; the alternative form is for use in circumstances when the first form may be thought inappropriate.

6 As a matter of principle the same basic form is provided for all occasions. The special variations for the Burial of a Child will be adapted at the minister's discretion according to the child's age and circumstances, bearing in mind the need for the whole service to be comparatively brief.

7 At times when it may be necessary or desirable to hold the service in the absence of the body, the Procession and Committal should be omitted. After the Lord's Prayer the minister should proceed to the prayers usually said after the Committal, and so end the service.

8 When a memorial service is held in addition to the Burial or Cremation, a different selection may be made from the psalms, lessons and prayers here provided. It is not appropriate to use the Commendation or Committal more than once in relation to the same person.

9 When the Words of Committal have already been said, it is not usual to conduct a further service at the time of the disposal of cremated ashes; but there are circumstances in which the minister may consider that such a service is appropriate. On such an occasion a psalm or lesson or both may be read, the ashes deposited or scattered, and prayers said. The psalm, lesson and prayers may be selected from those provided in the order of service which have not already been used.

The Service

The Minister, meeting the body and going before it, says one or more of these sentences, the people standing:

I am the resurrection and the life, says the Lord; he who believes in me, though he die, yet shall he live, and whoever lives and believes in me shall not die eternally.

Blessed are those who mourn, for they shall be comforted.

God so loved the world that he gave his only Son, that whoever believes in h'm should not perish but have eternal life.

The hour is coming, and now is, when the dead will hear the voice of the Son of God, and those who hear will live.

I am the good shepherd . . . My sheep hear my voice and I know them . . . and no one shall snatch them out of my hand.

Because I live, you will live also.

In the world you have tribulation; but be of good cheer, I have overcome the world.

The eternal God is your dwelling place, and underneath are the everlasting arms.

To thee, O Lord, I lift up my soul. O my God, in thee I trust.

God is our refuge and strength, a very present help in trouble.

He does not deal with us according to our sins, nor requite us according to our iniquities.

If we live, we live to the Lord, and if we die, we die to the Lord; so then, whether we live or whether we die, we are the Lord's. For to this end Christ died and lived again, that he might be Lord both of the dead and of the living.

Our Saviour Christ Jesus abolished death and brought life and immortality to light through the gospel.

2 A hymn may be sung.

3 One of these prayers may be said:
Let us pray.

Eternal God, the Lord of life, the conqueror of death, our help in every time of trouble, comfort us who mourn, and give us grace, in the presence of death, to worship you, that we may have sure hope of eternal life and be enabled to put our whole trust in your goodness and mercy, through Jesus Christ our Lord. **Amen.**

Heavenly Father, whose love is everlasting, help us now to turn to you with reverent and submissive hearts, that, through the steadfastness and encouragement that the Scriptures bring, we may have hope, and be lifted above our distress into the light and peace of your presence; through Jesus Christ our Lord.   **Amen.**

Almighty God, our refuge and strength, you have given us a High Priest who understands our human weakness. Help us therefore to trust in him and come with confidence to the throne of grace, that we may receive mercy and find grace in time of need, through Jesus Christ our Lord.
Amen.

The Ministry of the Word

4   The Minister may say:

We are met in this solemn moment to commend . . . . into the hands of Almighty God, our heavenly Father. In the presence of death Christians have sure ground for hope and confidence and even for joy, because the Lord Jesus Christ, who shared our human life and death, was raised again triumphant and lives for evermore.   In him his people find eternal life.   Let us then in humble trust hear the words of Holy Scripture.

5   This Psalm is said or sung:

Psalm 130

Out of the depths I cry to thee, O Lord!
Lord, hear my voice!
Let thy ears be attentive
to the voice of my supplications!

If thou, O Lord, shouldst mark iniquities,
Lord, who could stand?
But there is forgiveness with thee,
  that thou mayest be feared.

I wait for the Lord, my soul waits,
  and in his word I hope;
my soul waits for the Lord
  more than watchmen for the morning,
  more than watchmen for the morning.

O Israel, hope in the Lord!
For with the Lord there is steadfast love,
  and with him is plenteous redemption.
And he will redeem Israel
  from all his iniquities.

6   One or more of these Psalms may also be said or sung:

Psalm 23

The Lord is my shepherd,
  I shall not want;
he makes me lie down in
  green pastures.
He leads me beside still waters;
  he restores my soul.
He leads me in paths of righteousness
  for his name's sake.

Even though I walk through the
  valley of the shadow of death,
  I fear no evil;
for thou art with me;
  thy rod and thy staff,
  they comfort me.

Thou preparest a table before me
in the presence of my enemies;
thou anointest my head with oil,
my cup overflows.
Surely goodness and mercy shall
follow me all the days of my life;
and I shall dwell in the house of the
Lord for ever.

Psalm 103: 8-17

The Lord is merciful and gracious,
slow to anger and abounding in
steadfast love.
He will not always chide,
nor will he keep his anger for ever.
He does not deal with us according to our sins,
nor requite us according to our iniquities.
For as the heavens are high above the earth,
so great is his steadfast love toward
those who fear him;
As far as the east is from the west,
so far does he remove our transgressions
from us.
As a father pities his children,
so the Lord pities those who fear him.
For he knows our frame;
he remembers that we are dust.
As for man, his days are like grass;
he flourishes like a flower of the field;
for the wind passes over it, and it is gone,
and its place knows it no more.

But the steadfast love of the Lord is
    from everlasting to everlasting
    upon those who fear him,
    and his righteousness to children's children.

7   One or more of these passages of Scripture are read, the people
being seated.

John 14: 1-6, 27

'Let not your hearts be troubled; believe in God, believe
also in me. In my Father's house are many rooms; if it
were not so, would I have told you that I go to prepare a
place for you? And when I go and prepare a place for you,
I will come again and will take you to myself, that where I
am you may be also. And you know the way where I am
going.' Thomas said to him, 'Lord, we do not know
where you are going; how can we know the way?' Jesus
said to him, 'I am the way, and the truth, and the life; no
one comes to the Father, but by me.

Peace I leave with you; my peace I give to you; not as the
world gives do I give to you. Let not your hearts be
troubled, neither let them be afraid.'

1 Peter 1: 3-9

Blessed be the God and Father of our Lord Jesus Christ!
By his great mercy we have been born anew to a living
hope through the resurrection of Jesus Christ from the
dead, and to an inheritance which is imperishable, un-
defiled, and unfading, kept in heaven for you, who by
God's power are guarded through faith for a salvation
ready to be revealed in the last time. In this you rejoice,

though now for a little while you may have to suffer various trials, so that the genuineness of your faith, more precious than gold which though perishable is tested by fire, may redound to praise and glory and honour at the revelation of Jesus Christ. Without having seen him you love him; though you do not now see him you believe in him and rejoice with unutterable and exalted joy. As the outcome of your faith you obtain the salvation of your souls.

1 Corinthians 15: 1-4, 20-26, 35-38, 42-44, 50, 53-58

Now I would remind you, brethren, in what terms I preached to you the gospel, which you received, in which you stand, by which you are saved, if you hold it fast—unless you believed in vain. For I delivered to you as of first importance what I also received, that Christ died for our sins in accordance with the scriptures, that he was buried, that he was raised on the third day in accordance with the scriptures.

Christ has been raised from the dead, the first fruits of those who have fallen asleep. For as by a man came death, by a man has come also the resurrection of the dead. For as in Adam all die, so also in Christ shall all be made alive. But each in his own order: Christ the first fruits, then at his coming those who belong to Christ. Then comes the end, when he delivers the kingdom to God the Father after destroying every rule and every authority and power. For he must reign until he has put all his enemies under his feet. The last enemy to be destroyed is death.

But someone will ask, 'How are the dead raised? With what kind of body do they come?' You foolish man!

What you sow does not come to life unless it dies. And what you sow is not the body which is to be, but a bare kernel, perhaps of wheat or of some other grain. But God gives it a body as he has chosen, and to each kind of seed its own body.

So it is with the resurrection of the dead. What is sown is perishable, what is raised is imperishable. It is sown in dishonour, it is raised in glory. It is sown in weakness, it is raised in power. It is sown a physical body, it is raised a spiritual body.

I tell you this, brethren: flesh and blood cannot inherit the kingdom of God, nor does the perishable inherit the imperishable. For this perishable nature must put on the imperishable, and this mortal nature must put on immortality. When the perishable puts on the imperishable, and the mortal puts on immortality, then shall come to pass the saying that is written:
'Death is swallowed up in victory.'
'O death, where is thy victory?
'O death, where is thy sting?'

The sting of death is sin, and the power of sin is the law. But thanks be to God, who gives us the victory through our Lord Jesus Christ. Therefore, my beloved brethren, be steadfast, immovable, always abounding in the work of the Lord, knowing that in the Lord your labour is not in vain.

Romans 8:28, 31b-35, 37-39

We know that in everything God works for good with those who love him, who are called according to his purpose.

If God is for us, who is against us? He who did not spare his own Son but gave him up for us all, will he not also give us all things with him? Who shall bring any charge against God's elect? It is God who justifies; who is to condemn? Is it Christ Jesus, who died, yes, who was raised from the dead, who is at the right hand of God, who indeed intercedes for us? Who shall separate us from the love of Christ? Shall tribulation, or distress, or persecution, or famine, or nakedness, or peril, or sword?

No, in all these things we are more than conquerors through him who loved us. For I am sure that neither death, nor life, nor angels, nor principalities, nor things present, nor things to come, nor powers, nor height, nor depth, nor anything else in all creation, will be able to separate us from the love of God in Christ Jesus our Lord.

8 These or other passages of Scripture may be used: Psalm 90; 2 Corinthians 4: 16—5: 10; Revelation 7: 9-17; Revelation 21: 1-7.

9 A Sermon may be preached.

10 The Apostles' Creed may be said.

I believe in God, the Father almighty,
creator of heaven and earth.

I believe in Jesus Christ, his only Son, our Lord.
He was conceived by the power of the Holy Spirit
and born of the Virgin Mary.
He suffered under Pontius Pilate,
was crucified, died, and was buried.
He descended to the dead.
On the third day he rose again.
He ascended into heaven,
and is seated at the right hand of the Father.
He will come again to judge the living and the dead.

I believe in the Holy Spirit,
the holy catholic Church,
the communion of saints,
the forgiveness of sins,
the resurrection of the body,
and the life everlasting.   Amen.

Thanksgiving

11 The Minister says:

Let us pray.

Praise and honour, glory and thanks be given to you, almighty God, our Father, because in your great love for the world you gave your Son to be our Saviour, to live our life, to bear our griefs, and to die our death upon the Cross.

We praise you because you have brought him back from death with great power and glory, and given him all authority in heaven and on earth.

We thank you because he has conquered sin and death for us, and opened the kingdom of heaven to all believers.

We praise you for the great company of the faithful whom Christ has brought through death to behold your face in glory, who join with us in worship, prayer and service.

For your full, perfect and sufficient gift of life in Christ all praise and thanks be given to you for ever and ever.
Amen.

12 This or other prayers may be said:

Eternal God, in your wisdom and grace you have given us joy through the lives of your departed servants. We thank you for them and for our memories of them.

We praise you for your goodness and mercy that followed them all the days of their lives, and for their faithfulness in the tasks to which you called them.

We thank you that for them the tribulations of this world are over and death is past, and we pray that you will bring us with them to the joy of your perfect kingdom; through Jesus Christ our Lord.   **Amen.**

13   A hymn may be sung.

Commendation

14   The people standing, the Minister says:

Let us pray.

Merciful God, you have made us all and given your Son for our redemption. We commend our *brother* (*. . . . .) to your perfect mercy and wisdom, for in you alone we put our trust.   **Amen.**

15   The Lord's Prayer

Our Father . . .

16   When the whole service takes place in a crematorium chapel the Minister proceeds immediately to the Committal.

* Baptismal Name

F14

17   Otherwise the Minister may say:

> May the God of peace, who brought again from the dead our Lord Jesus, the great shepherd of the sheep, by the blood of the eternal covenant, equip you with everything good that you may do his will, working in you that which is pleasing in his sight, through Jesus Christ, to whom be glory for ever and ever. **Amen.**

---

18   The Minister going before the body to the grave, or at the crematorium, may say one or more of these sentences:

> As a father pities his children, so the Lord pities those who fear him. For he knows our frame; he remembers that we are dust.

> The Lord is good to all, and his compassion is over all that he has made.

> Blessed be the God and Father of our Lord Jesus Christ, the Father of mercies and God of all comfort, who comforts us in all our affliction.

> To this end Christ died and lived again, that he might be Lord both of the dead and of the living.

> We know that if the earthly house of our tabernacle be dissolved, we have a building from God, a house not made with hands, eternal, in the heavens.

Committal

19 When the body is laid in the earth or on the catafalque, the
people standing, the Minister says:

EITHER

Forasmuch as our *brother* has departed out of this life,
and Almighty God in his great mercy has called *him* to
himself, we therefore commit *his* body to the ground,
earth to earth, ashes to ashes, dust to dust (*OR*, to the
elements, ashes to ashes, dust to dust), in sure and certain
hope of the resurrection to eternal life through our Lord
Jesus Christ, to whom be glory for ever and ever. **Amen.**

OR

Forasmuch as our *brother* has departed out of this life,
we therefore commit *his* body to the ground, earth to earth,
ashes to ashes, dust to dust (*OR*, to the elements, ashes to
ashes, dust to dust), trusting the infinite mercy of God,
in Jesus Christ our Lord. **Amen.**

20 Then the Minister says:

I heard a voice from heaven saying, From henceforth,
blessed are the dead who die in the Lord; even so, says
the Spirit; for they rest from their labours.

21 Let us pray.

Merciful God, our heavenly Father, who made your Son
Jesus Christ to be the resurrection and the life, raise us,
we pray, from the death of sin to the life of righteousness;
that when we depart this life we may with this our *brother*
be found acceptable to you; for the sake of your Son,
Jesus Christ our Lord, who lives and reigns with you in
the unity of the Holy Spirit, one God world without
end. **Amen.**

These prayers may also be said:

> Father of all, we pray for those whom we love, but see no longer. Grant them your peace; let light perpetual shine upon them; and in your loving wisdom and almighty power work in them the good purpose of your perfect will; through Jesus Christ our Lord. **Amen.**

> Almighty God, Father of all mercies and giver of all comfort, deal graciously with those who mourn, that they may cast every care on you and know the consolation of your love; through Jesus Christ our Lord. **Amen.**

> Holy Father, grant us, in all our duties your help, in all our perplexities your guidance, in all our dangers your protection, and in all our sorrows your peace; through Jesus Christ our Lord. **Amen.**

> The grace of our Lord Jesus Christ, and the love of God, and the fellowship of the Holy Spirit, be with you all evermore. **Amen.**

Additional Prayers

One or more of these prayers may be said in place of those at the beginning of the Service:

> Father of mercies and God of all comfort, you have made nothing in vain and you love all that you have made. Look in tender pity on your bereaved servants, and help them by your grace to find in you their refuge and their strength. **Amen.**

Almighty God, always ready to forgive, no prayer is offered to you in vain. Speak to us your word of consolation, and in our sorrows draw us closer to yourself, so that in doing your will we may know your righteousness and mercy. **Amen.**

Almighty God, fountain of all wisdom, to whom our needs are known, have compassion on us, and mercifully give us those things we are not worthy to ask and those things we are too blind to know we need, for the sake of your Son, Jesus Christ our Lord. **Amen.**

One or more of these prayers may be used instead of, or in addition to, the prayers after the Committal. When the Service is said in church they may be used immediately before the Commendation.

Almighty and everlasting God, Lord of the living and the dead; give to the living mercy and grace; to the dead, rest and light perpetual. Give to your Church truth and peace; and to us sinners penitence and pardon; through Jesus Christ our Lord. **Amen.**

May God in his infinite love and mercy bring the whole Church, living and departed in the Lord Jesus, to a joyful resurrection and the fulfilment of his eternal kingdom.

Amen.

O God, whose mercies cannot be numbered; let your Holy Spirit lead us in holiness and righteousness; in the communion of the whole Church; in the confidence of a sure faith; in the strength of holy hope; in favour with you our God, and in perfect charity with all men; through Jesus Christ our Lord. **Amen.**

O God, the strength of the weak, the comfort of the sorrowful, the friend of the lonely; let not sorrow overwhelm your children, nor anguish of heart turn them from you. Grant that in the patience of hope and the fellowship of Christ they may continue in your service and in all godly living, until at length they also attain to fullness of life before your face; through Jesus Christ our Lord. **Amen.**

O God of infinite compassion, look in love and pity on your sorrowing servants. Be their support, their strength, and their shield; that they may trust in you and be delivered out of their distresses; through Jesus Christ our Lord. **Amen.**

Grant, Father, to the bereaved, the Spirit of faith, that they may receive your promised grace to help in time of need. May they look to Jesus, the pioneer and perfecter of faith, who for the joy set before him endured the Cross, despising shame, and is seated at your right hand in glory. As they return to the duties of life, let your peace protect them and the risen victorious Lord sustain them in your service all the days of their life. **Amen.**

The Burial or Cremation of a Child

At the burial or cremation of a child the Minister may, at *his* discretion, make these changes in the Service:

Psalm 23 may be said in addition to, or instead of, Psalm 130.

Even on occasions when it may be desirable that the Lessons should be as brief as possible, John 14: 1-6, 27 should be read, and also Mark 10: 13-16:

> They were bringing children to Jesus, that he might touch them; and the disciples rebuked them. But when Jesus saw it he was indignant, and said to them, 'Let the children come to me, do not hinder them, for to such belongs the kingdom of God. Truly, I say to you, whoever does not receive the kingdom of God like a child shall not enter it.' And he took them in his arms and blessed them, laying his hands upon them.

At the Committal this form may be used:

> Forasmuch as this child is in the care of Almighty God, we therefore commit *his* body to the ground, earth to earth, ashes to ashes, dust to dust (*OR*, to the elements, ashes to ashes, dust to dust), in sure and certain hope of eternal life, through our Lord Jesus Christ. **Amen.**

> The Lamb in the midst of the throne will be their shepherd, and he will guide them to springs of living water; and God will wipe away every tear from their eyes.

These prayers may be used instead of, or in addition to, the prayers provided after the Committal:

Lord Jesus Christ, you care for little children in this present life and have prepared for them in the life to come a home where they behold your Father's face. Make us assuredly to know that you have received . . .* in peace. For you have said, Let the children come to me, for to such belongs the kingdom of heaven. To you, with the Father and the Holy Spirit, be all glory, honour and worship, now and ever, world without end. **Amen.**

Almighty God, giver of every good and perfect gift, we thank you for the happiness and love this child has brought and for the assurance we have that *he* is in your care. Strengthen us to commit ourselves to your gracious providence, so that we may live our lives here in the peace and joy of faith, until at the last we are united with all the children of God in the brightness of your glory, through Jesus Christ our Lord. **Amen.**

*The child's Christian name

Another version of
The Apostles' Creed

I believe in God the Father Almighty,
maker of heaven and earth:

And in Jesus Christ his only Son our Lord,
who was conceived by the Holy Ghost,
born of the Virgin Mary,
suffered under Pontius Pilate,
was crucified, dead, and buried,
he descended into hell;
the third day he rose again from the dead,
he ascended into heaven,
and sitteth on the right hand of God the Father Almighty;
from thence he shall come
to judge the quick and the dead.

I believe in the Holy Ghost;
the holy Catholic Church;
the Communion of Saints;
the Forgiveness of sins;
the Resurrection of the body;
and the Life everlasting.   Amen.

The Ordination of Ministers also called Presbyters

If it is desired, the Sermon may be preached not after the Gospel but after the giving of the Bible.

The Ministry of the Word

1   This or some other hymn:

> The Saviour, when to heaven he rose,
> In splendid triumph o'er his foes,
> Scattered his gifts on men below,
> And wide his royal bounties flow.
>
> Hence sprung th' apostles' honoured name,
> Sacred beyond heroic fame;
> In lowlier forms, to bless our eyes,
> Pastors from hence, and teachers rise.
>
> From Christ their varied gifts derive,
> And fed by Christ their graces live;
> While, guarded by his mighty hand,
> Midst all the rage of hell they stand.
>
> So shall the bright succession run
> Through the last courses of the sun;
> While unborn churches by their care
> Shall rise and flourish large and fair.

Jesus our Lord their hearts shall know—
The Spring whence all these blessings flow;
Pastors and people shout his praise
Through all the round of endless days.

2   The Collect

Let us pray.

Almighty God, our heavenly Father, we thank you that in
every generation you give Ministers to your Church, so
that through them you may nourish and sustain its life and
equip your people for your service.   And we pray that
through the faithful work of those whom you have called
into this Ministry, your Church may be continually
strengthened to glorify your Name and to do your will.
We ask this through Jesus Christ our Lord.   **Amen.**

The Collect of the Day when used may follow or precede this
Collect.

3   The Old Testament Lesson

The book of Isaiah, the sixth chapter, beginning at the
first verse.
In the year that King Uzziah died I saw the Lord sitting
upon a throne, high and lifted up; and his train filled the
temple.   Above him stood the seraphim; each had six
wings: with two he covered his face, and with two he
covered his feet, and with two he flew.   And one called to
another and said:
'Holy, holy, holy is the Lord of hosts;
the whole earth is full of his glory.'

And the foundations of the thresholds shook at the voice of him who called, and the house was filled with smoke. And I said: 'Woe is me! For I am lost; for I am a man of unclean lips, and I dwell in the midst of a people of unclean lips; for my eyes have seen the King, the Lord of hosts!'

Then flew one of the seraphim to me, having in his hand a burning coal which he had taken with tongs from the altar. And he touched my mouth, and said: 'Behold, this has touched your lips; your guilt is taken away, and your sin is forgiven.' And I heard the voice of the Lord saying, 'Whom shall I send, and who will go for us?' Then I said, 'Here am I! Send me.'

4   The Epistle

The Letter of Paul to the Romans, the twelfth chapter, beginning at the first verse.

I appeal to you therefore, brethren, by the mercies of God, to present your bodies as a living sacrifice, holy and acceptable to God, which is your spiritual worship. Do not be conformed to this world but be transformed by the renewal of your mind, that you may prove what is the will of God, what is good and acceptable and perfect.

For by the grace given to me I bid every one among you not to think of himself more highly than he ought to think, but to think with sober judgment, each according to the measure of faith which God has assigned him.

For as in one body we have many members, and all the members do not have the same function, so we, though many, are one body in Christ, and individually members one of another.

Having gifts that differ according to the grace given to us, let us use them: if prophecy, in proportion to our faith; if service, in our serving; he who teaches, in his teaching; he who exhorts, in his exhortation; he who contributes, in liberality; he who gives aid, with zeal; he who does acts of mercy, with cheerfulness.

Let love be genuine; hate what is evil, hold fast to what is good; love one another with brotherly affection; outdo one another in showing honour. Never flag in zeal, be aglow with the Spirit, serve the Lord. Rejoice in your hope, be patient in tribulation, be constant in prayer.

5   This or some other hymn:

Lord, if at thy command
The word of life we sow,
Watered by thy almighty hand,
The seed shall surely grow:

The virtue of thy grace
A large increase shall give,
And multiply the faithful race
Who to thy glory live.

Now then the ceaseless shower
Of gospel blessings send,
And let the soul-converting power
Thy ministers attend.

On multitudes confer
The heart-renewing love,
And by the joy of grace prepare
For fuller joys above.

The Gospel according to John, the twentieth chapter, beginning at the nineteenth verse.

The people may say: **Glory to Christ our Saviour.**

On the evening of that day, the first day of the week, the doors being shut where the disciples were, for fear of the Jews, Jesus came and stood among them, and said to them, 'Peace be with you.' When he had said this, he showed them his hands and his side. Then the disciples were glad when they saw the Lord. Jesus said to them again, 'Peace be with you. As the Father has sent me, even so I send you.' And when he had said this, he breathed on them, and said to them, 'Receive the Holy Spirit. If you forgive the sins of any, they are forgiven; if you retain the sins of any, they are retained.'

Now Thomas, one of the twelve, called the Twin, was not with them when Jesus came. So the other disciples told him, 'We have seen the Lord.' But he said to them, 'Unless I see in his hands the print of the nails, and place my finger in the mark of the nails, and place my hand in his side, I will not believe.'

Eight days later, his disciples were again in the house, and Thomas was with them. The doors were shut, but Jesus came and stood among them, and said, 'Peace be with you.' Then he said to Thomas, 'Put your finger here, and see my hands; and put out your hand, and place it in my side; do not be faithless, but believing.' Thomas answered him, 'My Lord and my God!' Jesus said to him, 'Have you believed because you have seen me? Blessed are those who have not seen and yet believe.'

The people may say: **Praise to Christ our Lord.**

G5

7   The Sermon

8   The Nicene Creed

> **We believe in one God,**
> **the Father, the Almighty,**
> **maker of heaven and earth,**
> **of all that is, seen and unseen.**
>
> **We believe in one Lord, Jesus Christ,**
> **the only Son of God,**
> **eternally begotten of the Father,**
> **God from God, Light from Light,**
> **true God from true God,**
> **begotten, not made,**
> **of one Being with the Father.**
> **Through him all things were made.**
> **For us men and for our salvation**
> **he came down from heaven:**
> **by the power of the Holy Spirit**
> **he became incarnate from the Virgin Mary, and was**
>   **made man.**
> **For our sake he was crucified under Pontius Pilate;**
> **he suffered death and was buried.**
> **On the third day he rose again**
> **in accordance with the Scriptures;**
> **he ascended into heaven**
> **and is seated at the right hand of the Father.**
> **He will come again in glory to judge the living and the dead,**
> **and his kingdom will have no end.**
>
> **We believe in the Holy Spirit, the Lord, the giver of life,**
> **who proceeds from the Father and the Son,**
> **With the Father and the Son he is worshipped and glorified.**

He has spoken through the Prophets.
We believe in one holy catholic and apostolic Church.
We acknowledge one baptism for the forgiveness of sins.
We look for the resurrection of the dead,
and the life of the world to come.   Amen.

The Presentation

9   The Secretary of the Conference presents to the President those
who are to be ordained Presbyters, saying:

Mr President, I present to you these persons to be ordained
Ministers. They have been examined and found to be of
sound learning and devout life.   The Conference has
received them into Full Connexion and resolved that they
be ordained by prayer and the imposition of hands.

Then the Secretary reads the names of the candidates for
Ordination, each candidate rising as his or her name is called,
and remaining standing.

The people also stand, and the President says:

Beloved in Christ, these are the persons whom we intend,
in God's name, to ordain to the Ministry of his Church in
the Order of Presbyters. We therefore ask you to declare
your assent to their Ordination. Do you believe that they
are by God's grace worthy to be ordained?

The people answer: **They are worthy.**

The Examination

10 The people sit, and the President says to those who are to be
    ordained, still standing:

> Brethren and sisters, the Church is the family of God, the
> body of Christ, and the temple of the Holy Spirit. All
> who are baptized are called to make Christ known as
> Saviour and Lord, and to share with him in the renewing
> of his world. You are called to the ordained Ministry
> within the ministry of the whole Church. It will be your
> task as ambassadors on behalf of Christ to preach the
> Gospel by word and deed, to declare God's forgiveness to
> penitent sinners, to baptize, to confirm, to preside at the
> celebration of the Sacrament of Christ's Body and Blood,
> to lead God's people in worship and prayer, to care for
> them in sickness and in health, to teach them and to equip
> them for their service. You must set the Good Shepherd
> before you as your pattern. Seek and serve his sheep that
> are scattered abroad, for whom he laid down his life; that
> they may be saved through Christ for ever. See that no
> member of Christ's flock suffers hurt through your neglect.
> Never cease from your work of love until you have done
> all in your power to bring them to full obedience to Christ.
>
> This ministry will make great demands on you and your
> household: the power to fulfil it is the gift of God alone.
> Pray earnestly therefore for the Holy Spirit. We trust that
> you are determined by God's grace to give yourselves
> wholly to his service, devoting to him all your powers of
> mind and spirit, and sharing with his people in their
> common witness to the world.

Brethren and sisters, do you believe that you are called by God to this office and work?

Answer: I do.

Do you accept the Holy Scriptures as containing all things necessary for eternal salvation through faith in our Lord Jesus Christ?

Answer: I do.

Do you believe the doctrines of the Christian faith as this Church has received them?

Answer: I do.

Will you accept the discipline of this Church and work together with your brethren and sisters in its ministry?

Answer: I will.

Will you be faithful in prayer and in the reading of the Holy Scriptures and in those studies which will help you to understand and expound them?

Answer: I will.

May the Lord who has given you the will to do these things give you the grace and power to perform them. **Amen.**

The Ordination

11 The President says to the people:

Beloved in Christ, let us first pray earnestly for these persons before we send them forth to the work for which we believe they have been called by the Holy Spirit.

Let us pray.

All pray in silence.

The President sums up the prayers of the people, saying:

God our Father, you have promised to hear the prayers of those who pray in the name of Christ: grant that what we have asked in faith may be granted to us according to your will, through Jesus Christ our Lord. **Amen.**

12 Hymn

Come, Holy Ghost, our souls inspire,
And lighten with celestial fire;
Thou the anointing Spirit art,
Who dost thy sevenfold gifts impart:

Thy blessèd unction from above
Is comfort, life, and fire of love;
Enable with perpetual light
The dullness of our blinded sight:

Anoint and cheer our soilèd face
With the abundance of thy grace:
Keep far our foes, give peace at home;
Where thou art guide no ill can come.

Teach us to know the Father, Son,
And thee, of both, to be but One;
That through the ages all along
This, this may be our endless song:

All praise to thy eternal merit,
O Father, Son, and Holy Spirit!

Amen.

13 The ordinands kneel, and the President, standing, says:

> God and Father of all, we praise you for your infinite love
> in calling us to be a holy people, a royal priesthood, a
> universal Church; and in giving us your Son Jesus Christ
> our Lord to be the Head of the Church and the Shepherd
> of our souls.
>
> We thank you that by his death he has overcome death,
> and having ascended into heaven has abundantly poured
> forth his gifts; making some apostles, some prophets, some
> evangelists, some pastors and teachers; to equip your people
> for the work of ministry and the building up of his body.
> We thank you that you have now called these your servants
> to this same ministry; and therefore we pray that they
> may receive the gifts which they need for their calling.

Here the President lays *his* hands upon the head of each
ordinand in turn, other Ministers also laying on their right
hands.

The President says over each one:

> Father, send the Holy Spirit upon *N.*, for the office and
> work of a Minister in the Church of Christ.

Each time the President says this prayer, the people answer:

> **Amen.**

When *he* has laid *his* hands on all of them, the President
continues:

> Father, grant that these your servants may continually
> grow in grace and faithfully fulfil their ministry. May they
> watch as true pastors over those entrusted to their care.
> May they boldly proclaim the gospel, rightly administer

the sacraments, and with all your people offer spiritual sacrifices to you and service to all mankind. Give them patience and skill in teaching, wisdom in giving counsel, loyalty in working with others. Keep them blameless in their ministry, so that they may be called at the last, with all your faithful servants, to enter into your eternal joy: through Jesus Christ your Son our Lord, who with you and the Holy Spirit is alive and reigns, one God, for ever and ever.

The people say:

Amen.

14 The Lord's Prayer

Our Father . . .

15 The President gives a Bible to each of the new Ministers.

16 The President says:

Seeing that you have been duly ordained by prayer and the imposition of hands, I declare in the Name of our Lord Jesus Christ, the only Head of the Church, that you have authority to preach the Word of God and to administer the holy sacraments as a Minister in the Church of Christ.

Be shepherds to the flock of Christ. Hold up the weak; bind up the broken; bring again the outcasts; seek the lost. So be merciful that you are not too remiss; so minister discipline that you forget not mercy: that when the Chief Shepherd appears you may receive the never-fading crown of glory, through Jesus Christ our Lord. **Amen.**

The Lord's Supper

17 The Peace

The President says:

>The peace of the Lord be always with you.

>**And also with you.**

18 The President proceeds to the Lord's Supper, beginning at the
Setting of the Table, during which this or some other hymn is sung:

>**Behold the servant of the Lord!**
> **I wait thy guiding eye to feel,**
>**To hear and keep thy every word,**
> **To prove and do thy perfect will,**
>**Joyful from my own works to cease,**
>**Glad to fulfil all righteousness.**

>**Me, if thy grace vouchsafe to use,**
> **Meanest of all thy creatures, me:**
>**The deed, the time, the manner choose,**
> **Let all my fruit be found of thee;**
>**Let all my works in thee be wrought,**
>**By thee to full perfection brought.**

>**My every weak, though good design,**
> **O'errule, or change, as seems thee meet;**
>**Jesus, let all my work be thine!**
> **Thy work, O Lord, is all complete,**
>**And pleasing in thy Father's sight;**
>**Thou only hast done all things right.**

Here then to thee thy own I leave;
  Mould as thou wilt thy passive clay;
But let me all thy stamp receive,
  But let me all thy words obey,
Serve with a single heart and eye,
And to thy glory live and die.

                                        Amen.

19 After the post-communion prayer, the President says this
    prayer:

> Look graciously, Father, upon these whom you have now
> made your Ministers, and grant that in the Church, at
> home, and in the world they may be examples to us of
> Christian faith and love. Grant that with them we may
> serve you and rejoice in your glory all our days; through
> Jesus Christ your Son our Lord. **Amen.**

20 This or some other hymn:

> O thou who camest from above
>   The pure celestial fire to impart,
> Kindle a flame of sacred love
>   On the mean altar of my heart!
>
> There let it for thy glory burn
>   With inextinguishable blaze;
> And trembling to its source return,
>   In humble prayer and fervent praise.
>
> Jesus, confirm my heart's desire
>   To work, and speak, and think for thee;
> Still let me guard the holy fire,
>   And still stir up thy gift in me.

Ready for all thy perfect will,
　My acts of faith and love repeat,
Till death thy endless mercies seal,
　And make the sacrifice complete.

　　　　　　　　　　　　　　　Amen.

21　The President then concludes the service.

The Lord's Prayer

EITHER:

Our Father, who art in heaven,
hallowed be thy Name;
thy kingdom come;
thy will be done;
on earth as it is in heaven.
Give us this day our daily bread.
And forgive us our trespasses,
as we forgive those who trespass against us.
And lead us not into temptation;
but deliver us from evil.
For thine is the kingdom,
the power, and the glory,
for ever and ever.   Amen.

OR:

Our Father in heaven,
hallowed be your Name,
your kingdom come,
your will be done,
on earth as in heaven.
Give us today our daily bread.
Forgive us our sins
as we forgive those who sin against us.
Do not bring us to the time of trial
but deliver us from evil.
For the kingdom, the power, and the glory
    are yours
now and for ever.   Amen.

Complete ecumenical agreement has not been reached about a modern version of the
Lord's Prayer. The form printed in the booklets which preceded this Service Book is
replaced by the above form, which now has greater acceptance.

July 1975